I Am the Christ

[AN IN-DEPTH LOOK AT
THE SPIRITUAL QUALIFICATIONS
OF JESUS AND A CAREFUL EXAMINATION
OF THE RESURRECTIONS TO COME]

Stephen Marshall Barber

Copyright © 2022 by Stephen Barber

All rights reserved. No part of this publication may be reproduced, distributed or transmitted in any form or by any means, including photocopying, recording, or other electronic or mechanical methods, without the prior written permission of the publisher, except in the case of brief quotations embodied in critical reviews and certain other noncommercial uses permitted by copyright law. For permission requests, write to the publisher, addressed "Attention: Permissions Coordinator," at the address below.

Barber/New Harbor Press
1601 Mt. Rushmore Rd, Ste 3288
Rapid City, SD 57701
www.newharborpress.com

I /Stephen Barber —1st ed.
ISBN 978-1-63357-264-5

Editors: Sheila Anne Barber and Manny Miranda

Scripture quotations marked (NLT) are taken from the Holy Bible, New Living Translation, copyright © 1996, 2004, 2007 by Tyndale House Foundation. Used by permission of Tyndale House Publishers, Inc., Carol Stream, IL 60188. All rights reserved.

Scripture quotations marked "NASB" are taken from the NEW AMERICAN STANDARD BIBLE®, Copyright © 1960, 1962, 1963, 1968, 1971, 1972, 1973, 1975, 1977, 1995 by The Lockman Foundation. Used by permission.

Scripture quotations marked "KJV" are taken from the Holy Bible, King James Version (Public Domain).

Contents

Introduction 1

Chapter 1: I Am the God of Creation 13

Chapter 2: I Am the Good Shepherd 39

Chapter 3: I Am the Resurrection 67

Chapter 4: The Resurrection of the Dead 93
    [The Loss]

Chapter 5: The Resurrection of the Dead 117
    [The Judgment]

Chapter 6: The Resurrection of Life 139

Chapter 7: I Am the Salvation of God 173

Bibliography 201

About the Author 203

Introduction

TODAY, THE CHURCH APPEARS to have lost its urgency to announce the good news of the Gospel. The Church just does not seem interested in taking a public stand for Christ. Yet, there are people dying every day, sealing their fate without Jesus Christ. In fact, eternity is approaching the entire world at an alarming rate, and the stakes are extremely high. And still the church remains largely silent. Why? Where is the biblical precedence for this position of indifference? It's no wonder the world has lost its respect for the Bible. Obviously, the Church does not respect the Bible either. It isn't using the Bible as its own blueprint for life. Why should the world?

    The Church must remember that Christ never remained silent; he spoke the truth even in the face of great opposition. He lived and died by the Word of God. And the world flocked to hear him speak. They were captivated by his words of life. Therefore, it makes me wonder why the Church has taken this position of silence. Has the Church forgotten the words of life? If the Church really wants to be heard, if the Church really wants to be Christ-like, it must take a stand and begin living in the light of God's Word. We must walk as Christ walked and speak as he spoke. Once that becomes a reality, then the Church will have something worth proclaiming, and the Good News of the Gospels will ring out. And the world will hear.

In short, the Church cannot afford to adhere to society's moratorium on biblical input. The truth must be spoken. Yet, how many churches will be willing to strengthen or develop a viable outreach ministry designed to reach the unchurched? How many churches will be willing to focus their energies on a discipleship program where every church member is trained and prepared to share their reason for believing in Jesus Christ?

This book was written with simple goals in mind. The first goal was to motivate churches into being more assertive in telling the world about Jesus and the approaching judgment. The world has the right to know the truth, and, if churches are too unwilling to stand up right now, then maybe this little book might encourage them to stand and proclaim the truth. The world needs to know the spiritual fitness of Jesus Christ. Jesus came to lead everyone into the presence of God, and everyone who fails to follow Jesus' leadership will never enter into eternal life.

Based upon the reality of Jesus Christ, the reader has been provided with a short but intense look at Jesus Christ. Who was Jesus? Was he special? Did he have a message that we need to hear? The book starts out by examining the qualifications of Jesus Christ, outlining his role in creation, exploring his capacity to lead, and delving into the power of the Resurrection that resided within him. The first part of the book is designed to provide the reader with an in-depth look at Jesus. After all, people deserve to know who God is demanding that we believe in, who God expects us to trust in, and who God sent to save us. The world has the right to know who they can turn to for their spiritual needs.

The book begins with an introduction of Jesus as a co-creator of creation. The entire ninth chapter of the Gospel of John was devoted to this one purpose. The world needed to know that the God of creation had humbled himself by becoming a part of his own creation. Jesus entered the world in human-likeness (Philippians 2:7). He took our humanity upon himself; in so doing, we could talk one-on-one and face-to-face with God. God was willing to get personal. Jesus brought divinity into our world (Philippians 2:6). Jesus walked among us; God walked among us. Jesus was the blending of humanity and divinity into one person—himself. He could represent man and God. He became the perfect mediator between man and God (1 Timothy 2:5). He was a divine gift in human likeness for our benefit.

Next, the reader will encounter Jesus as the Good Shepherd (John 10:11). The world has the right to know if Jesus was actually qualified to lead or not. Therefore, this chapter examines the ministry of Jesus. Did he demonstrate the necessary leadership traits? Did Jesus appear to be someone in whom we could trust? Would our soul be safe in his keeping? Questions like these are addressed through the second chapter. This is not an area where the world needs to be guessing. Direct assurance is absolutely necessary. Jesus would have to demonstrate the correct heart—a heart oriented toward the betterment of all humanity to qualify as a true spiritual leader. Anything short of that would have disqualified him as the Good Shepherd. Therefore, the words and deeds of Jesus have been placed under a microscope for the benefit of the reader.

Now that everyone knows who the Good Shepherd is, Jesus provides the reader with a front row seat through the resurrection of Lazarus. The story begins by allowing everyone to know that Lazarus was a personal friend of Jesus, and the account also informs everyone that Jesus loved his friend (John 11:3). Yet, Jesus allowed his friend to die; Jesus simply stood by allowing the death of his friend to occur (John 11:4–6). Although Lazarus' death actually occurred in the manner explained in this chapter, Jesus had ample reasons for not intervening (John 11:11–15). By waiting for Lazarus' death, Jesus could showcase many of the different aspects of the coming resurrection. No doubt, the costs for this demonstration were high, but the benefits for doing so were eternal, impacting all of humanity. God's love for all humanity compelled Jesus not to intervene. One must remember that there can be no resurrection without a death first occurring. However, the story does not end with death having the final word. The story ends with Lazarus rising from the dead and people realizing that Jesus was and is the fulfillment, the essence, and the reality of the Resurrection (John 11:25). Jesus held the power of life in his hands, and he still does today. That is the message contained in the eleventh chapter of the Gospel of John.

The first half of the book has but one design: to remove all doubts, objections, and concerns concerning Jesus' fitness to be God's messenger of life. The Scriptures clearly point out that Jesus was one of the co-creators of humanity. The Son of God was there in the beginning (John 1:1–14). We were made in his image (Genesis1:26–27); he has a vested interest in us. In addition, the Scriptures outline Jesus' spiritual qualifications as the Good Shepherd. Not only did he have a part in our creation, now through the resurrection, he would have a part in our redemption as well. Jesus demonstrated his love for us over and over again (Romans 5:8). There is simply no one more qualified.

With Jesus firmly established as the pivotal point that determines which resurrection every person will face, the book examines the reality of each resurrection and the characteristics associated with each one. It cannot be overstressed: The end of time is approaching. This means that the judgment of God is approaching as well (Acts 17:31). Everyone needs to be cognizant of the different resurrections that are coming, and into which of the two very different resurrections an individual will most likely find themselves facing.

Which of the resurrections an individual will face should not be a mystery; there are just too many indicators signaling which resurrection an individual is approaching (Galatians 6:7–10).

Introduction

In other words, there will be no surprises; everyone has been provided with more than enough advanced warnings. Everyone lives their life in the shadow of the warnings associated with each resurrection (Galatians 6:8). Distinct road signs have been posted, indicating the final destiny for each person. After all, there are but two roads available. One leads to life, and it is marked with road signs that indicate life. The other road leads to death, and it is marked with road signs warning every traveler of their end.

Therefore, no one can claim ignorance as to where they are headed. Everyone can detect their destiny by observing the road signs they are passing each day. A sign indicating that one is heading north means that one is heading north. Signs that indicate that one is heading south means that one is heading south. Both roads are adequately marked; both roads are posted so as to remove any possible error as to their intended destiny. Likewise, the road heading toward death is littered with warnings (John 3:18, Galatians 5:21, Revelation 20:11–15). If a person does not like the road signs he or she is seeing, they are free to make a U-turn at any time (Acts 2:38). In fact, both roads share one thing in common: U-turns are legal. People can make a U-turn anywhere they want without fear of incurring a penalty. Indeed, U-turns are encouraged on the south-bound–death-bound lanes.

Now, let's look at the two different resurrections. One resurrection is for the *damned*—those whose names are not found written in the Book of Life. The other resurrection is for the *redeemed*—those whose names are found written in the Book of Life (Revelation 20:11–15). Both resurrections share some common features. Both are sure to take the breath away from all who enter, and both have one-way doors. In other words, once you enter there is no turning back. Both are eternal in nature; they are never-ending. The entrance to both resurrections is determined at the cross of Christ. Membership in the resurrection of the redeemed is based on the acceptance of Jesus' sacrifice, and the other resurrection is based upon the rejection of Jesus' sacrifice (Mark 16:16). Both resurrections are the product of choice. Both are determined on an individual basis; no one can make the choice for another person (Romans 10:9). Both choices are therefore very personal. No one will be able to blame someone else for where they spend eternity, but this is where the common features end. From this point onward, the differences between the two resurrections begin to overshadow their shared common features.

The resurrection of the dead is a fate that need not be encountered by any man or woman (Matthew 25:41). God has gone to great lengths to prevent this outcome (Luke 19:10), but so many insist on a world without God (Romans 1:18–19). God even sent his only Son in an effort to extricate everyone from being sent to this terrible place. The final destiny of the damned is so appalling that one chapter could not adequately describe its dreadful features. Therefore, the topic of the resurrection of the dead was divided into two separate chapters, allowing the two major themes associated with the resurrection of the dead to be sufficiently addressed.

The first chapter of the resurrection of the dead will deal with the utter loss that every participant will incur (Matthew 25:29–30). This loss will be catastrophic and unimaginable. The reason the loss is so difficult to imagine is because everyone currently lives in a world impregnated with elements of life (Genesis 1:31). At every turn we encounter life-giving moments, and we should not be surprised at this situation. God created everything, and he made life rich (Genesis 1:26–31). But, it must be remembered that God is the God of the living (Matthew 22:32). He is not the God of the dead, and everyone who enters into the resurrection of the dead will no longer reside in a land blessed by the presence of God. They will be disowned by God (Matthew 7:23). Simply put, the dead have no God. As a result, every life-giving moment and life-giving element will cease—forever. There will be no God

Introduction

to sustain life. The eternally dead will never encounter life-giving elements—ever again. Life will be over—ended—terminated.

They will know only a complete and total loss of everything. There will be no sunrises or sunsets; there will only be an unending darkness (Matthew 22:13). There will be nothing to see; there will be no trees blowing in the wind, no sound of running water in the creeks, no birds chirping. Every sound of life will be silenced—forever gone. Time will have no meaning. Buried alive will take on a whole new and horrifying meaning. The eternally dead will be beyond hope or grace or even mercy (Luke 19:24–25). There will be no one to hold their hands or to look into their eyes or to hear their cries. Their only companion will be the never-ending darkness, for they exist in a place with no God. No one living could have imagined this desolate lifeless place. Those who reject Christ reject life (Matthew 10:33, Luke 10:16, John 12:48). Those who despise Christ despise life. Christ and his servants warned people to avoid the place of judgment (Matthew 5:29, Romans 2:3–11); hell was never created for humans. It was created for Satan and his demons (Matthew 25:41).

In the second chapter of the resurrection of the dead, the reader will investigate the approaching judgment of God. Everyone needs to remember that with every passing day the judgment draws nearer and nearer; its arrival is unavoidable. As terrible as that day will be, it will also be a good day. For, on that day, Satan and his demonic hoard will come face-to-face with the unbridled wrath of God. Their wicked rule will end; their ability to bring torment and pain to the world will cease.

The crop of destruction sown by Satan and his demons will be ready for harvest. It will be a harvest overflowing with misery and pain. Simply stated, hell was designed and created for them; hell was to be their eternal abode. Please remember and never forget that hell was never designed for humanity. Jesus came into our world in the likeness of man so that he could redeem all of humanity from the wrath of God (John 3:36, Romans 5:9, 1 John 4:10). In other words, God provided everyone with a way to escape the coming judgment (2 Corinthians 5:21, 1 Thessalonians 5:9). Jesus laid down his life that we might live (John 15:13). Jesus paid the cost for our pardon; he purchased our freedom from death with his own blood (1 Peter 3:18). He was crucified that we might live (1 John 2:2). There is no reason for any man or any woman to share in Satan's fate. God had other plans for his creation—and it is called *redemption*.

The redemption of the world was the reason God sent his Son into the world; Jesus came to intervene (Hebrews 9:12). The Son of God came to square off with evil. He came to conquer the unconquerable. He stood when we could only fall. The cost for humanity's redemption would be high, but the Son of God came despite the cost; he endured the opposition, the mocking, the scourging, the pain, and the shame because he dared to love (Hebrews 12:2–3). Jesus came to bridge the gap between man and God (1 Timothy 2:5–6).

Eternity with God will be full of life, wonder, and awe (John 8:12). Every attribute, every characteristic, every quality of God will be experienced. God's presence will cause every aspect of life to be amplified into one fluid moment followed by yet another and another and another. Humans will know the richness of God; we will experience the oneness shared between God the Father, God the Son, and God the Holy Spirit. Life will never be boring; our exploration of God's divine nature will never cease. The supernatural will become our new world. The unbelievable will become the believable. The unimaginable will light up our new life. We will stand in the eternal light of God (John 8:12).

There is another key point that must not be overlooked. Currently the redeemed are living at the lowest point they will ever know; they share an existence in a sin-distorted world with the damned, but that will all change. Equally important is the fact that the damned are living at the highest point they will ever experience. There is coming a time when the damned will depart from this sin-distorted world (Matthew 22:12). They will enter into a place designed for Satan and his demons. The damned will never again see or touch a world impregnated with life—ever again. The damned will enter into a land of "weeping and gnashing of teeth" (Matthew 22:12). In contrast, the redeemed will stand in the eternal presence of the One who created all life, and there they will live forever.

Jesus unequivocally stated that he was the only way to God, he was the truth, and he was the life: "No one can come to the Father except through me" (John 14:6). According to Jesus, there are no other pathways to God. That means that all other gods and their respective religions are quite literally dead-ends. None of them have the power to lead anyone into the eternal presence of God. There is no salvation outside of Jesus Christ.

Jesus was the common ground between man and God. By the will of God, Jesus was both human and divine. He entered our world through a virgin (Matthew 1:18–25). His life came through the power of the Holy Spirit (Matthew 1:18). No other person has ever been both human and divine. Jesus was the only one who had the right and the power to act on humanity and God's behalf. Jesus was the perfect mediator between God and humans. Jesus was sent into the world for this very purpose. He came to lay down his life that others might live (John 10:11).

"The highway to hell is broad, and its gate is wide for the many who choose the easy way. But the gateway to life is small, and the road is narrow, and only a few ever find it" (Matthew 7:13–14). Jesus' death upon the cross "is the power of God at work saving everyone who believes" (Romans 1:16).

> For if you confess with your mouth that Jesus is Lord and believe in your heart that God raised him from the dead, you will be saved. For it is by believing in your heart that

you are made right with God, and it is by confessing with your mouth that you are saved. (Romans 10:9–10)

Jesus claimed to be God, and his claim "must be either true or false" (McDowell, 1999, p. 159). It cannot be both true and false; either Jesus was God, or he was a liar—a fraud. However, if Jesus was God in the flesh, everyone must respond to God's offer. There is no choice; everyone must decide how important or unimportant Jesus is to them. That leaves everyone with but two options. One, an individual can trust God and accept forgiveness for their sins through the work of Christ. Or, an individual can reject or neglect God's provision. The reason for the rejection will not matter in the end because the reason for the rejection will not have the power to alter the eternal consequences. Everyone who rejects Christ will spend an eternity in a devil's hell.

God has made his offer of life open to everyone (John 12:46–47), and everyone has the power to accept or reject God's offer (John 12:46–48). This book was written to assist everyone in their decision-making process. No one should make an uninformed decision; there is simply too much at stake. One's soul is too important and eternity is an unlimited, unmeasurable amount of time. To put it differently—and more accurately—to be condemned to a devil's hell is to be sent into a place of utter judgment where time is not a factor. Satan's eternal torment does not come with an expiration date—it will never end—it will go on and on and on throughout all eternity. Once the second death starts, it will never end.

There is no salvation outside of Jesus. Only Jesus had the endorsement of God. "And a voice from heaven said, 'This is my beloved Son, and I am fully pleased with him'" (Matthew 3:17). The Bible is true. "The godly will inherit the land and will live there forever" (Psalm 37:29), but the wicked have no future (Psalm 37:38).

Introduction

It is perfectly clear then that this is the testimony that Jesus wanted to bear of Himself. We also see that the Jews must have understood His reply as a claim to His being God. There were two alternatives to be faced then; that His assertions were pure blasphemy or that He was God. (McDowell, 1999, p. 140)

We must either embrace Jesus' claim that He is God's Son or reject it. There is no intellectually honest alternative, given Jesus' claim that He is the only solution to bridge the gap between our sinfulness and God's holiness: "I am the way, and the truth, and the life; *no one comes to the Father but through Me*" (John 14:6). (Jeffress, 2017, ps. 200–201)

It is my hope that the simple message contained within this book will be heard. The book was designed to be clear and easy to understand, enabling everyone to make an informed decision about Jesus Christ. The eternal destiny of everyone is being written every day. We are either writing a story of life or a story of death. Each person is their own author daily writing the ending of their story. Please read what you have already written. A few moments of introspection won't kill you, and it could help you determine how you want to proceed with your story. You may even decide to change the ending of your story. After all, you and I have the freedom to edit our own work.

My story is simple. I will believe in God's Son. Jesus is standing beside the Father, and he is holding my future in his hand. I will enter heaven by the grace of God. I will do so because the blood of Christ separated me from my sin. I am a sinner saved by the grace of God. Jesus Christ died for me, and I trust in his work.

If anyone has a loved one, a friend, or a coworker who does not know Christ as their savior, the time to correct that is running out. If you are someone who does not know Christ as your Savior, your time to correct that is also running out. The time for salvation is now. Everyone needs to act wisely with the little time that is left. Christ is but one prayer away. Eternal life with God is but one prayer away. God will not reject the humble. Pray while you still can; pray while you can still be heard. As long as you draw breath, you are living in the time of grace.

Do not abuse God's grace. Jesus stepped within time and died for you and me. Now is the time to call upon Jesus for salvation. Obviously, this must be done from within time. Once death has occurred, the deceased individual has stepped outside of time and, therefore, beyond grace, and beyond forgiveness and beyond salvation. In the following chapters, the reader will begin to realize just how much weight truly rest upon their decision.

CHAPTER 1

I Am the God of Creation

(A Completion of Creation)

THE NINTH CHAPTER OF the Gospel of John has been misunderstood for hundreds of years. Consequently, the true message within this chapter has been lost. This tragic situation must not be allowed to continue. The Church of today needs to hear the same message that the original audience heard and received. I hope you will allow the original message contained in the ninth chapter of the Gospel of John to unfold as we travel through this rich chapter.

For the moment, with your patience, we will set aside the traditional understanding of Jesus healing the blind man. Allow the Scriptures—the words in each verse—to speak. Keep in mind that the Holy Spirit knew what he wanted to say and what he needed to convey. If we allow the Holy Spirit's choice of words to be heard, without any human interference, the true meaning can and will be heard.

Tradition is normally important because it should serve as a safeguard against heresy, but, in this rare case, the traditional understanding of healing is serving as a stumbling block to a proper understanding. Obviously, a true test of a good traditional understanding is whether or not it agrees with or is supported by the Scriptures it is supposed to be representing. If it isn't, the traditional understanding must be permanently rejected. And, in this case, the concept of healing does not agree with the wording in the ninth chapter of the Gospel of John.

Surely, everyone can remember the problem the Pharisees had with Jesus. The Pharisees valued their "man-made teachings" over the word of God (Mark 7:8). In fact, the Pharisees were so weighed down and distracted by their cherished traditions that they failed to see or hear God even when he stood right before their eyes. This was a catastrophic blunder.

In like manner, the Church of today may value traditional teachings, but we must at the same time acknowledge their limitations. Traditions are subordinate to the Scriptures, and, in some cases, they can serve as a safeguard, setting forth what has been declared in the Scriptures. In so doing, traditions are servants to the Scriptures—nothing more. It is imperative that everyone allows the Scriptures to speak, enabling the original message to surface.

When people perform exegesis, they look at Scripture and attempt to flesh out meaning based on the plain words, the genre, the context, and other scriptural references. They are not necessarily trying to force their own views on the text—and certainly should not be (Ham, 2013, p. 187).

The events recorded in the ninth chapter of the Gospel of John were intended to introduce Jesus as one of the original co-creators of humanity. In the beginning, God the Father, God the Son, and God the Holy Spirit created man in their image (Genesis 1:26–27). This fact was recorded in the Holy Scriptures, and it was completely understood and accepted by the Jewish people.

I Am the God of Creation

So, with that understanding firmly established in the Jewish mind, the Holy Spirit led Jesus to the man born blind. The people of God were about to watch one of the co-creators in action. Jesus would complete an act of creation as described in the Book of Genesis, and through this creative act, Jesus would receive a divine introduction. Jesus would stand in the light of the creation scriptures. God wanted the religious leaders to see Jesus through a creative lens/light. The Holy Spirit was weaving the creation account as recorded in Genesis and Jesus into one current event.

At this point in Jewish history, the disciples and the Jewish community were facing desperate times under Roman rule, and they were anticipating the arrival of their Messiah. The Scriptures foretold of his coming, and the Messiah would need a royal introduction. In particular, the introduction would need to be fit for a King. Obviously, only a divine introduction would do; it would have to be supernatural. It would need to be an introduction with Godlike, heaven like, otherworldly components. This divine introduction would need to single Jesus out as the only possible Messiah—God's true Messiah. Nothing short of the divinely supernatural would do. It would need to be something beyond the limits of humanity; it would need to be of Spirit origin.

Therefore, the Holy Spirit orchestrated an encounter between Jesus and a man who was born blind. Here stood the Son of God, as a man, doing what only God could do—an act of pure creation. The timing could not have been any better; it was divinely perfect. The Jewish leadership was currently anticipating the coming of a great Messiah. They knew the Messiah would be unique, perfectly endowed with the power from on high. The Messiah would be identified by doing those things that only God could do, and all they needed to do was to watch and wait for the supernatural to appear.

However, several stumbling blocks stood in the way of the Jewish leadership. First, they were anticipating a powerful military Messiah. According to their thinking, he would need to terminate the Roman occupation of Israel. The Jewish leadership had become blinded by their need to throw off the Roman oppression. Second, their Messiah would be expected to acknowledge, endorse, and support the supremacy of the pharisaical rule. The Jewish leadership had fallen into the trap of thinking that they were the guardians and rulers of righteousness. Third, the Jewish leadership had their traditions, their rules, and their ceremonies that the Messiah would need to affirm. They assumed the Messiah would comply with their established traditional system. In other words, their Messiah would comply with their spiritual understanding as it was; he would need to meet their expectations and dreams, and he would need to fit into their world. After all, their Messiah only needed to provide a little military muscle, a little divine intervention aimed at supporting their agenda. They already knew what needed to be done. They had everything figured out. Their Messiah would support their cause. He would line up with their plans. Their dreams would become fulfilled. They would recognize him because he would powerfully serve their cause.

The error being made by the Jewish leadership was simple: They assumed they knew just how God's power would be most effectively utilized. They were convinced by their own traditions that the most pressing need of the day was freedom from the Roman oppression, and any Messiah failing to gratify their program would meet firm opposition. In essence, they were demanding that the Messiah be made into their image. The power of God would need to fulfill the will of the Sanhedrin, exalting their supremacy. Their Messiah would be formed by their hands, by their ideas, and by their will. Sadly, Jesus was not their man.

Instead, Jesus' whole reason for coming was based upon the will of the Father—not the Sanhedrin. "Look, I have come to do your will, O God" (Hebrews 10:7). Jesus did not come as a worldly military leader. He did not come to crush the Roman tyranny. He did not come to embrace the agenda of the Jewish leadership, and he did not come to uphold their traditions. The stage for conflict was already firmly set. The lines had been drawn—Jesus and his message of redemption would not be expected. Jesus was simply too different from their expectations. The outcome was simple: The Son of God would be rejected. The Jewish leadership would choose not to see Jesus as God's Messiah. Jesus was simply not a Messiah of their making.

Furthermore, the Holy Spirit's introduction of Jesus would be the furthest thing from their minds. As we examine the ninth chapter of John, the reader will come to realize that the Scriptures were portraying Jesus according to God's plan and not according to the preconceived notions of the Jewish leadership. Jesus was God's provision for humankind. He was God's Messiah sent to redeem humanity. This redemption would be spiritual; it would reach further than the temporal goals of the Pharisees. Jesus was born for God's purposes, and he would walk out God's plan. Therefore, the introduction of Jesus would be in line with the Father's purposes. Jesus' introduction would be from the spiritual realm. Its purpose would be to introduce the divine, the infinite to the finite, and the finite would struggle with the width, the depth, and the height of the infinite.

Now, it is time for humanity to look upon the divine; God's Messiah had stepped upon the stage of history. "As long as Jesus is in the world He must reveal Himself in word and deed as the world's Light" (Tasker, 1989, p. 123). The long-awaited Messiah came demonstrating the power of God, but not in a militaristic manner as expected. Jesus came with a scriptural introduction; he came fulfilling the Scriptures, and, in so doing, the Scriptures singled him out and testified about his true identity. God's method was designed to illuminate the mind of the Jewish nation. With that said, let's begin our examination of the ninth chapter of the Gospel of John and explore the untold story that has been overlooked for hundreds of years.

Exploring the Untold Story

As we begin our study, several factors must be incorporated if an understanding aligned with the original intent is to be obtained. The first factor is the theme of the ninth chapter of the Gospel of John. What is the subject of the chapter? The answer to that question is the key to unlocking the original message. If properly identified, it will provide the correct filter or lens from which to process each part of the event. So let's begin by identifying the question the disciples were presenting to Jesus.

Jesus was walking along and he came across a man who was blind. The Scriptures do not outline any hint of a conversation that may or may not have taken place between Jesus and the blind man. All we know is that the disciples became curious; they wanted to know, "Why was this man born blind?" (John 9:2). Before Jesus could answer, they posed their own answer in the form of a question: "Was it a result of his own sins or those of his parents?" (John 9:2).

So, what were the disciples really questioning? What were they grappling with? What were the disciples struggling to understand? At first glance, it may appear the disciples were asking about the man's blindness, but a more prolonged contemplation reveals much more. The blind man's inability to see was only the occasion for the question and nothing more. The disciples' question ran much deeper. In essence, the disciples were asking: "Why was this man born blind when the majority of people are born with the ability to see?" Knowing that the majority of people were born with the gift of sight, the disciples were wrestling with the creative works of God. The Jewish people correctly attributed the crafting of the human body to be a work of God. They knew, beyond any doubt, that the act of creation was solely in God's domain. They believed the words recorded in the Psalms: "You made all the delicate, inner parts of my body and knit me together in my mother's womb" (Psalm 139:13).

The disciples were trying to understand what went wrong in this man's case. Why was he born blind? In addition, it is important to note that the disciples could not have posed their question to anyone more qualified. No one could provide more insight on creation than Jesus. After all, Jesus was in the beginning. He participated in creation with God the Father and God the Holy Spirit. The disciples were about to learn, to experience firsthand, about the direct link between Jesus and creation. This day the disciples would meet the real Jesus, the author of life. Before this encounter was over, this blind man would not be the only one to be given the gift of sight. All would see far more than they bargained for!

As I have said, the vast difference between the blind man and everyone else born with the gift of sight prompted the disciples questioning. "Why was this man born blind?" The disciples could never have anticipated as to where their question would have led them. In addition, they were over-confident with their assumption for the blindness. In fact, their presupposition for the man's blindness rendered them unable to see the real reason behind the man's blindness. This situation made the disciples just as blind as the blind man. So, let's return to their question: "Why was this man born blind?" Their original question remained, demanding an answer, and there was Jesus: ready, willing, and qualified to provide the right answer.

A majestic awe filled the atmosphere. Jesus guided his disciples right through the creation story, providing his disciples with a firsthand glimpse of the creative power of God. Jesus would peel back time, exposing what took place on the sixth day of creation. What no eye had ever seen would be seen. Second, Jesus would demonstrate that his "workmanship is marvelous," and that he is not restricted to weaving us "together in the dark[ness] of the womb" (Psalm 139:14–15). By publicly completing an act of creation, Jesus would shock the natural senses. Everyone standing there knew about the creative power of God through the Scriptures, but a current live performance of creation would not have been anticipated.

Remember, Jesus did not hesitate to rule out sin as the causing factor for the man's blindness. Jesus stated that sin was not the cause. Jesus basically swept aside the disciples' traditional mindset. A person's difficult circumstances were not always a clear sign of God's disapproval or the by-product of sinful actions. After sweeping aside the disciples' incorrect reason for the blindness, Jesus answered the disciples' question: "He was born blind so the power of God could be seen in him" (John 9:3).

I would like to slow down at this point and refer us to the King James rendering of the third verse which enhances a correct understanding of this passage: "Neither hath this man sinned, nor his parents: but that the works of God should be made manifest in him." This wording is extremely insightful: "but that the works of God should be made manifest in him." The word *but* was used by Jesus to tie his response back to the disciples' original question.

Jesus told the disciples that he would manifest or publicly complete a creative work of God, showcasing the creative power of God. In other words, this man's creation had not been completed in the womb; Jesus would provide the final touches of creation by publicly providing the gift of sight. Through Jesus' actions, the works of God, the creative works of God, would be placed on public display—open to the view of everyone. The complex gift of sight was accomplished with simplicity. Our response should be one of gratitude and wonder. "Thank you for making me so wonderfully complex! Your workmanship is marvelous . . . You watched me as I was being formed in utter seclusion, as I was woven together in the dark of the womb" (Psalm 139:14–15).

Stop and think for just a moment. As Jesus completed the final touches of creation, the disciples were being invited to watch the gift of sight as it was being added to the man who had been born blind.

> Then he [Jesus] spit on the ground, made mud with the saliva, and smoothed the mud over the blind man's eyes. He told him, "Go and wash in the pool of Siloam" (*Siloam* means "sent"). So the man went and washed, and came back seeing! (John 9:6–7)

Plainly, this once-in-a-lifetime gift of sight was not being completed in secret—in the womb. Quite the opposite, this gift of sight was publicly added, displaying or manifesting the creative power of God. In addition, the disciples were being invited to stroll through the Word of God right back to the sixth day of creation. The words recorded in the Book of Genesis were being lived out right before the eyes of everyone.

> And the Lord God formed a man's body from the dust of the ground and breathed into it the breath of life. And the man became a living person. Then the Lord God planted a garden in Eden, in the east, and there he placed the man he had created. (Genesis 2:7–8)

Jesus fulfilled the Genesis account of creation just as he had stated he would do a few moments earlier. The man was born without the gift of sight so that the creative works of God could be publicly displayed—not hidden in the womb as was the norm and not hidden by hundreds of years of history. This creative act would be accomplished in plain sight. This was a marvelous event designed to expand the disciples' vision of Jesus. Here, in tangible physical form, stood the God of Creation. Who else but God could complete an act of creation, demonstrating firsthand how man was originally created?

According to the Genesis account, dust was used to create life. Now, before the eyes of a watching crowd, Jesus once again stooped down, collected some dust, and added the creative power of God to provide the gift of sight. What was done on the sixth day of creation was publicly done by Jesus, fulfilling the Genesis model of creation. In the process, Jesus was introduced as a co-creator. Based upon the Scriptures, here stood the Messiah.

No one other than God had ever created life from dust. Normally, when someone gets dust into their eyes, the results are disruptive, but not in this case. This was a beautiful experience for the disciples and for anyone who happened to be standing nearby. Every time I read this account of the blind man, I'm reminded of these words: "Then God looked over all he had made, and he saw that it was excellent" (Genesis 1:31). Without question, the same can be said for what Jesus did. He added the final touch of creation and it was excellent. Obviously, this creative act herald Jesus as a co-creator of life.

> Since the Bible is God's Word to man, He must expect us to understand it. As such, it makes sense that He would communicate His message to us in such a way so that we can indeed comprehend it if we are serious about wanting to know the truth. (Ham, 2013, p. 228)

Jesus Personified the Word of God

Again, through this creative act, Jesus manifested the creative works of God and he brought the Genesis account of creation forward in time. Jesus was reminding us of how we began. In the beginning, when God created Adam and Eve, God did so without the use of the womb. God formed Adam from the dust of the ground (Genesis 2:7). God used his hands to form Adam. Have you ever tried to form dust? You can't until you introduce a wetting agent. That is what Jesus did in this account.

He added his saliva to the dust to make mud. Then, he mixed in the creative power of God, and the formerly blind man could see. And Jesus did all of this without the use of the womb just as Adam was formed without the use of a womb. Jesus was following the Genesis' account of creation. God's methodology in this instance had but one purpose: to form a bond between what Jesus was doing and the Genesis account of creation. This connection would stand as a means of introducing Jesus as a co-creator. Jesus personified the Word of God. That was the reason Jesus fulfilled the Genesis account of creation. In so doing, an Old Testament creation spotlight was directed upon Jesus' current work, highlighting the creative aspect of Jesus' work.

At this point, I would like to introduce a factor that should shed light onto a proper understanding of this whole event. It is found in the very words of Jesus himself: "Don't misunderstand why I have come. I did not come to abolish the law of Moses or the writings of the prophets. No, I came to fulfill them" (Matthew 5:17). So, how does one fulfill the Scriptures? What should we see when someone is fulfilling the Scriptures? Jesus fulfilled the Scriptures by completing or complementing their message, by elaborating on their meaning, by converting written expressions into real-life actions, and by physically embodying the divine concepts contained in the Word of God. The Holy Spirit was making the Word of God come alive through the actions of the Son. The Holy Spirit was conveying the simple fact that Jesus was the personification of the Scriptures (John 1:1–5). In other words, the life spoken of in the Scriptures and the life in Jesus were one and the same. The words in the Scriptures found their expression in the actions of Jesus.

Normally, one must pray for God's guidance, read a passage, and then pray again, asking God to enlighten the mind. Next, one must meditate upon the possible meaning of the passage. Then, one must search the Scriptures for a correct interpretation. Finally, one must go before God again, listening for the Holy

Spirit to confirm the accuracy of the understanding. But, in this creative case, Jesus personally embodied the Genesis account. He modeled man's original creation. Through Jesus' actions everyone was allowed to see the total agreement between the written Word of God and the living Word of God. In other words, Jesus demonstrated the oneness shared between himself and the Scriptures—there was perfect unity between the Genesis account and Jesus' live performance. Jesus fulfilled the Genesis account of creation.

The Reason Jesus Fulfilled the Scriptures

Now that we know what it means to fulfill the Scriptures and the impact it can have on one's understanding, we ask: "Why did Jesus come to fulfill Scriptures? What was the purpose in doing so?" Simple! Each time Jesus fulfilled a specific passage, that passage demonstrated the unity between Jesus and the written Word of God. This allowed various scriptures to highlight different aspects of his divine character, providing the disciples with a continually developing all-encompassing vision of Christ. This was the process whereby the Holy Spirit provided a divine picture of who Jesus really was—the Son of God. He was God's chosen Messiah. In addition, the continual fulfillment of the Scriptures by Jesus allowed the Scriptures to bear witness toward his identity. The Scriptures were testifying, magnifying, proclaiming the uniqueness of Jesus as the Son of God and as the Messiah.

This interaction between Jesus and the Scriptures should have been obvious, even expected. Just as there is a oneness shared between God the Father, God the Son, and God the Holy Spirit, there is also a oneness shared between God and his Word. That oneness was being revealed each and every time Jesus fulfilled a passage of Scripture. God was taking the written Word of God, which the nation held as sacred—something to be trusted, and he was using that one sacred thing to reveal his Son. Jesus was quite literally standing in the light of God's Word. Jesus was being singled out. The Scriptures were separating Jesus from the crowd. What greater testimony could God have provided Jesus? None! God provided his Son with his best testimony. God was giving his Word—that which he had stood by for centuries. He was giving his Son the best introduction he could provide. Jesus' introduction was divinely supernatural. It incorporated God's name: It carried his honor. There was simply no better endorsement available. The Great I Am was standing behind his Son.

The light of the Scriptures was the brightest light God could have directed upon his Son. It is ironic to realize that the Israelites had possessed the very light that God would use to reveal his Son. They held and safeguarded that light for hundreds of years. And yet, the leadership claimed that the evidence was not good enough (John 9:29). Was the light too dim? The more Scriptures Jesus fulfilled, the greater the testimony, the greater the light. The bond between Jesus and the written Word of God was growing stronger and brighter. According to the Scriptures, Jesus was the Son of God. Remember, Jesus came to fulfill the Scriptures. He came to transform the written word into living expression. The truth walked among us, he spoke to us, and he ate with us. And finally, he died for us, leaving us a record of his life. The truth about Jesus is written.

This powerful bond between Jesus and the written Word of God left the Jewish leadership with but two options. One, they could acknowledge Jesus as God and accept his leadership, or they could reject him. But, if they opted for rejection, they had to deny the working of the Holy Spirit because the Spirit was weaving a powerful bond between the Old Testament and Jesus. Again, this process placed the Jewish leadership in a precarious position. Obedience or rebellion lay at their doorstep. Anyone seeking truth would be blessed by what Jesus did and said, but anyone demanding truth to conform to their personal standards and expectations or anyone trying to protect their own position or interest would end up in opposition to God. The same reality stands true today. We must allow the Scriptures Jesus fulfilled to illuminate our understanding of his actions as recorded in the New Testament.

There was no reason why everyone present couldn't have seen the declaration being made by God: This is my Son. This is your God! This is your Messiah! "I am fully pleased with him" (Matthew 3:17). Yet, as we travel through the story, you will see that the truth turned out to be too much for a large portion of the Jewish leadership. God's Messiah was not fitting into their image. According to them, Jesus would need to demonstrate his power according to their expectations. They were insisting on Jesus fulfilling their plans. According to them, Jesus needed to bring freedom from the hated Roman rule, he needed to follow their traditions, and he needed to acknowledge their leadership. Their hardheartedness was dangerous. They were unwilling to bend; their lack of humility left them unyielding.

Jesus came to follow God's plan—not the Sanhedrin's. It had been God's plan not to finish the creation of the blind man while he was still in his mother's womb. It was God's plan for Jesus to provide the finishing touch of creation. Jesus was following the will and the plan of God. So, in truth, the Jewish leaders were having a problem with God the Father, not the Son. Jesus was following the lead of his Father. It is important to note that it was Jesus who first saw the blind man. "As Jesus was walking along, he saw a man who had been blind from birth" (John 9:1). It was Jesus who paused and looked intently at the blind man. Jesus was always looking for the presence of his Father, and his goal was to finish the Father's work (John 4:34).

Returning to our story in the ninth chapter of the Gospel of John, we find Jesus looking at the blind man. We do not know how long Jesus actually looked at him, but it was long enough for the disciples to begin pondering the man's blind condition.

Jesus knew their questions would come. This was not a chance meeting. Jesus had been walking through his day, looking for the presence of his Father. Upon seeing the blind man, he knew what he was supposed to do; he would finish his father's work. It would be a learning experience for everyone else. When Jesus was finished, there should have been no further objections as to who he was. This beautifully executed plan was flawless. Everyone would see!

It should be noted: There was no healing power in the clay, only the creative power of Jesus Christ. Jesus displayed his glorious power; a power that had resided in him from the very beginning. After applying the clay to the man's eyes, Jesus instructed the blind man to go wash, and, as a result, the formerly blind man could see (v. 7). Many were astounded, and they wanted to know how his eyes were opened (v. 8–10). It is important to note that no one asked how his eyes were healed. They asked how his eyes were opened. The formerly blind man described the process of Jesus turning dust into clay, and how, after following Jesus' instructions, his blindness was gone (v. 11). This account stirred the interest of the Pharisees. The creative account must have sounded familiar; it must have had a divine ring to it. Therefore, the Pharisees inquired further, hungry for more details concerning how the man had gained his sight. The sharp ears of the Pharisees could detect the biblical method of creation when the man said: "He smoothed the mud over my eyes, and when it was washed away, I could see!" (v. 15).

The Pharisees were well-versed in the Old Testament, and Jesus had just completed an act of creation based upon the Genesis model. Only a willfully blind Pharisee would be unable to see the spiritual significance. As a result, a great division arose among the Pharisees. Jesus was a paradox. According to the majority of the Pharisees, Jesus had repeatedly failed to uphold their traditions. Yet, Jesus continually fulfilled biblical text, and he was therefore supported with continued biblical endorsement again and again, and again. Jesus' actions brought the Pharisees to a crossroad—a crossroad that had no middle ground.

The Pharisees had but two options. First, they could bow down and acknowledge Jesus as God's chosen Messiah, and follow his lead. This option would most likely result in a major change in their recognition and power among the people. Or, the Pharisees could reject Jesus. After all, he was the one who continually broke their traditional teachings. There was simply no middle ground for the Pharisees. Someone would have to give ground. The main issue between Jesus and the Pharisees was one of power. Who would bow down and acknowledge whom? This latest creative miracle of Jesus was powerful. It was God-like. It catapulted Jesus to the top. Jesus had used the dust of the earth to create a component of life.

Obviously, if the Pharisees acknowledged this creative act and the connection it held to the Genesis account, they would be acknowledging Jesus as their long-awaited Messiah. And the Pharisees would lose position, power, and prominence. They would decrease, and Jesus would increase. In essence, they would be following in the footsteps of John the Baptist (John 3:30). This unimaginable loss of power would prove to be too much for many of the religious leaders. With no middle ground between Jesus and themselves, they would have to do the unthinkable. Just as King Saul would not give way to David, the Pharisees would not give way to Jesus. The Pharisees' unwillingness to let go of their traditions led to their willingness to reject Jesus. The right choice had been found unacceptable.

The Pharisees claimed to be looking for the Messiah, but here was God's chosen Messiah standing right before them clothed in the creative power of God. Nevertheless, they chose poorly, and their choice pitted them against God. The guardians of righteousness, unwilling to bow down, would now become the enemies of righteousness. The Pharisees' chosen path would result in them denying Jesus' divinity and denouncing the source of Jesus' power. They would have to reject the harmony between Jesus and the Scriptures. They would have to reject the witness of the Holy Spirit. They would have to murder the Son of God—all in the name of self-preservation. The stakes were high and they were devastatingly eternal. The Pharisees would reap a bitter harvest. They would forfeit the opportunity to personally interact with God. They were throwing away the privilege of speaking with God—man to man. They could have touched God! They could have sat down and eaten dinner with God. They could have looked into his eyes, and enjoyed the warmth of his smile. They could have picked his brains and shared precious moments. The leadership of the chosen nation was on the precipice of forfeiting an intimate relationship with the Son of God. The opportunity to be known and to know God was being aborted. They were cutting God out of their lives.

Unfortunately, they were severing themselves from the Bread of Life. The Pharisees were ignoring a vital question that needed to be answered: "But, how could an ordinary sinner do such miraculous signs?" (v. 16). If the Pharisees had answered that one question, it would have turned their rebellion into obedience. Their legacy would have been a beacon of light and not a shadow of death. Not willing to embrace the truth, they had to search for a justifiable reason to reject God's provision.

With pressure mounting, the Pharisees once again questioned the man who had been blind and demanded of him, "This man who opened your eyes—who do you say he is?" (v. 17). The Pharisees are questioning the formerly blind man as to the origin of Jesus. This is a pure act of desperation. The Pharisees are attempting to reject the testimony of all the scriptures Jesus has fulfilled in the Torah, and they are turning to one who has no spiritual authority for spiritual insight. Now, that makes sense! Reject Jesus, who has consistently demonstrated the presence of God, but please listen to the formerly blind man who has done nothing but beg for his entire life. The formerly blind man knew but one thing for sure; he was blind, and now he could see. As to whom Jesus was, he could not provide a definitive answer. Nevertheless, the facts were enough for him. The wonder of the miracle did not hinge on his opinion of the one who had opened his eyes. However, the situation wasn't so simple for the Pharisees. "The Jewish leaders wouldn't believe he had been blind" (v. 18). Why? Because it was self-serving! It would be far easier to refute a state of blindness than to reject a creation miracle. Therefore, the Pharisees needed to search further into the situation, and their search led them to the parents of the formerly blind man. However, the man's parents were very careful as to how they answered the questions presented to them, knowing that anyone who acknowledged Jesus as the Christ would most likely be put out of the synagogue (vs. 20–22).

Subsequently, the man's parents affirmed the change in their son's condition, but pleaded ignorance as to how the change occurred. They were unwilling to take a stand. Their son would have to stand on his own. So, once again the man was questioned, and once again he was unwilling to budge from his original answer. He remained faithful to his original testimony (vs. 24–25). The man simply would "not be bullied into accepting a judgment about Jesus" (Tasker, 1989, p. 124). It is important to note that the questioning was directed heavily toward the method Jesus used, and less toward validating the miracle itself. Clearly, the Genesis methodology was troubling the religious leaders. Could they deny Jesus and not deny the Word of God?

The Pharisees needed to be able to separate Jesus from the scriptural testimony of the Genesis account. However, their continued stubbornness was bringing them deeper into dangerous territory. The next few passages record just how spiritually dangerous the situation had become for the Pharisees. In verse 27, the formerly blind man—with no regard for himself—challenged the reasoning behind the continued questioning. "'Look!' the man exclaimed. 'I told you once. Didn't

I Am the God of Creation

you listen? Why do you want to hear it again? Do you want to be his disciples, too?'" It was apparent that the Pharisees were struggling with Jesus' alignment with the creation account. The connection between Jesus and Genesis was very disturbing, but it was rock solid. The Pharisees were torn between their need to reject Jesus and their loyalty toward God's Word. Under extreme pressure, the religious leaders lashed out at the formerly blind man: "We know God spoke to Moses, but as for this man, we don't know anything about him" (v. 29).

Undeniably, the response that followed from the formerly blind man was the fulfillment of Mark 13:11, which says: "But when you are arrested and stand trial, don't worry about what to say in your defense. Just say what God tells you to. Then it is not you who will be speaking, but the Holy Spirit." The formerly blind man spoke freely as he was directed. He did not attempt to defend himself. His situation was not his concern. He mounted no defense for himself; he never tried to protect himself in any way. The man freely allowed the Holy Spirit to speak through him. In so doing, the Pharisees were not disputing with the man, but with the Holy Spirit. The Pharisees heard the truth whether they liked it or not. The formerly blind man was beautifully obedient. Not only were the religious leaders arguing with the Holy Spirit, but they were rejecting the Holy Spirit's testimony. And, if the Jewish leadership threw the man out of the synagogue, they would actually be throwing the Holy Spirit out.

> The man [the Holy Spirit] answered and said to them, "Well, here is an amazing thing, that you do not know where He is from, and yet. He opened my eyes. We know that God does not hear sinners, but if anyone is God-fearing, and does His will, He hears him. Since the beginning of time it has never been heard that anyone opened the eyes of a person born blind. If this man were not from

God, He could do nothing.' (John 9:30–33, New American Standard)

The Holy Spirit's testimony contained two important facts. First, the miracle performed was unusual; it had never been accomplished before in human history. Second, the inability of the religious leaders to recognize Jesus' right-standing with God, and his unquestionable obedience to God was the product of a choice—not based upon a lack of evidence as claimed by the Jewish leadership. The religious leaders were rejecting spiritual evidence that had been provided by the Holy Spirit. And the Holy Spirit declared the evidence to be sufficient; their refusal to acknowledge the truth did not diminish the reality of the situation.

Interestingly, at this point, the religious leaders made the same inappropriate judgment that the disciples had made at the beginning of the chapter. They attributed the man's blindness to sin (v. 34). When Jesus heard that the formerly blind man had been cast out, he searched for him (v. 35). Upon finding him, Jesus freely revealed his divine identity to the man, and as a result, the man believed in Jesus as the Christ. In the end, the formerly blind man lost nothing, and he gained everything. He had truly received his sight, and Jesus spoke with him. "Then Jesus told him, 'I have come to judge the world. I have come to give sight to the blind and to show those who think they see that they are blind'" (v. 39, New Living Translation). Those who refused to see the truth were made blind by their own unwillingness to acknowledge Jesus as the Christ. Unfortunately, the spiritual blindness of the latter was the result of sin, whereas the formerly bind man's lack of sight was not the result of sin.

Obviously, the message of God in this passage was clearly centered on Jesus as a cocreator of life. The Redeemer had stepped out onto the stage of human history. The world would never be the same. The Scriptures foretold of his coming. However, he would be rejected by many. But those humble enough to accept Jesus would have eternal life (John 3:16). The focus of John chapter nine was toward that end.

Creation Is the Theme

Jesus was God's spiritual provision for man. He had the power to complete an act of creation outside of the womb just as he had the power to create within the womb. Adam and Eve are the two prime examples of God creating without the use of a womb. However, there had been no living man around to observe that act of creation, but in this situation all that changed. Before the eyes of everyone, Jesus stooped down and took the dust of the earth and mixed it with a wetting agent and made clay. He formed the clay over the man's eyes, providing the gift of sight. From this creative act, everyone could see just how personal the original creation of humankind really was. God formed Adam in a like manner. It was personal. It was hands-on, and it was intimate. Then God formed the woman from the side of Adam, and allowed Adam the privilege of naming his new mate. She would be called Eve.

In the beginning of the story, Jesus stated the truth when he declared that sin was not the cause of the man's blindness. Nothing was wrong, and nothing had gone wrong in the man's creation. The man's creation had simply not been completed, allowing Jesus to furnish the finishing touch of sight. It was important for Jesus to demonstrate, model, and provide an example of his divine creative power. God the Father used the Book of Genesis and the creation account of Adam as a means to authenticate his Son. The message was clear. According to the Holy Spirit, enough evidence had been presented.

There is no language in John chapter nine that refers to a healing of any kind. There are many other passages throughout the Bible that deal with Jesus' willingness and ability to heal, but this is not one of those passages. As noted by Leon Morris, a clergyman and author of numerous books, there are more accounts of Jesus restoring sight to the blind than any other type of healing (1989, p. 475). Jesus had the power to heal; that is not being disputed.

The ninth chapter of John should not be stripped of its God-given message of creation just because Jesus did heal many people. The ninth chapter of the Gospel of John was the Father's introduction of Jesus as a co-creator. God wanted everyone to know that Jesus predated the beginning of humankind. And, therefore, the ninth chapter of John should not be titled or referred to as the chapter where Jesus healed the man who was born blind. The work accomplished in this story goes much deeper and broader than a "simple" healing. Creation was the main theme at the beginning of the chapter, and it remained the main theme throughout the chapter. Jesus never changed the topic. The creation theme runs through the entire chapter.

The glory of this chapter is found in its original Holy Spirit-inspired message, and the chapter should be free to declare its God-intended message. Jesus came to fulfill the Scriptures, and he artfully displayed his rightful place in the Trinity as the Son of God as he turned dust into a component of life. Jesus demonstrated the creative powers of God before everyone.

From a strictly human perspective, the formerly blind man was the only person who had a legitimate reason to want to reject God. He had spent so many years waiting for the moment when he would see. He never realized that he was waiting for his creator to personally come and finish his creation. Yet, he was the one who was willing to boldly testify in the face of great opposition. He would not back down from the truth, and neither should we. We should follow the formerly blind man's example. He testified boldly when the religious leaders were searching desperately for a reason to reject Jesus.

This story ends with an element of joy and sadness. The formerly blind man who could not see in the beginning gained both physical and spiritual sight. The religious leaders, who held the Scriptures to be divine, should have seen Jesus as God's provision based upon the spiritual evidence. The testimony provided was overwhelming. Their spiritual blindness should have given way to sight, but they would have nothing to do with it. They preferred their blindness out of self-preservation.

The Old Testament Scriptures fulfilled by Jesus provided important insights. As I have shown, they testified, clarified, and defined exactly what Jesus was doing, and just how unique Jesus was. He was the Son of God. He was God in the likeness of humanity. The Old Testament creation passages Jesus incorporated and fulfilled highlighted and reinforced the case for creation. This event offered everyone the opportunity to see the Son of God participating in the creation of life. Blindness could be traded in for sight. God, quite literally, offered the best introduction possible. God shined a divine spotlight on his Son; he confirmed his Son's identity using the established Word of God.

Considering all the spiritual evidence presented, I would like you to remember the following points. First, the disciples were questioning creation at the beginning of the story. Second, the Holy Spirit connected the Genesis account of creation with Jesus. And last, the Old Testament passages on creation defined the type of work Jesus was accomplishing.

Take the time to read Genesis chapters one and two. Then reread the entire ninth chapter of the Gospel of John, allowing the Scriptures to speak freely. You will see the relationship shared between these passages. God knew what he wanted to say, and how it needed to be said. The Old Testament passage the Holy Spirit incorporated into the ninth chapter of John does not support the concept of healing, but it does support a concept of creation. There are numerous Old Testament passages that refer to God's willingness to heal, yet none of them were incorporated into the ninth chapter of the Gospel of John. Why? The answer is simple. John chapter nine has nothing to do with the concept of healing.

Jesus completed an act of creation, and it established him as a co-creator. His introduction was beautifully orchestrated. This would free man from looking any further for the Messiah. Jesus was obviously working hand-in-hand with the Father, bringing the plan of salvation to fruition. We must strive to see and hear what the original audience saw and heard, or we risk losing the intended message contained in the ninth chapter of the Gospel of John. I hope you can see.

Looking back over the events that transpired, we can accurately follow the topic of discussion. The topic of creation was set by the disciples, and the creation topic was never changed by Jesus. Therefore, the only proper lens for an accurate interpretation of the events is a creation lens. It puts everything into perfect perspective, facilitating an opportunity to grasp a proper understanding of the story as it unfolds. With a creation lens, we can see what the disciples saw. With a creation filter, we can hear what the disciples heard, and we can stand right beside the disciples, experiencing the creative power of God firsthand. God's creative works were on display. With the aid of this creation event, we can picture God creating Adam; we can see Adam's form taking shape. We can see God's care and attention to every detail. We can rejoice in God's workmanship, how his thoughts guided his hands during our creation. We are a living, breathing, thinking expression of an eternal God. God is worthy of our praise. We should stand in awe of him. He gave us the gift of sight, and he opened our eyes right along with the man who had been born blind. I hope you can see with clarity the reality of this creation story.

According to John 9:3, the works of God would be publicly displayed in the blind man. And that is exactly what happened. First, Jesus revealed what took place on the sixth day of creation when Adam was created. No one was there at the time to observe this act of creation, but Jesus displayed how it unfolded through the formerly blind man. Second, Jesus revealed that God is the author of what is done within the womb. Even though babies are formed hidden from the sight of man, God is the creator of life (Psalm 139:13–15). Jesus quite literally gave everyone the ability to see the past creative works of God and the continuing creative works of God through the formerly blind man. According to the Holy Spirit, Jesus' demonstration was sufficient (John 9:30–33).

CHAPTER 2

I Am the Good Shepherd

(John 10)

JESUS CLEARLY STATED IN the tenth chapter of the Gospel of John: "I am the good shepherd" (v. 11). His statement eliminated all others; Jesus was the only one who could lead others to God. According to Jesus, he was the one and only Good Shepherd. No one but God is "good" (Matthew 19:17). Jesus was uniquely qualified to lead. Only he could guide others into the eternal presence of God because: "He was with God and he was God" (John 1:1). No one else on Earth knew the way. Jesus was the great "I Am," and he was willing to take on the likeness of man and personally shepherd man out of the darkness and into the light (John 10:9–13). Only Jesus had come from above (John 8:23); his origin was not of the earth, and he was fully capable of speaking about heavenly things (John 3:31). He had no equal, nor did he have any worthy rivals; he was the "Good Shepherd."

Jesus came to Earth, the dwelling place of humans, to save mankind from the coming judgment. In the process, he validated his status as the Good Shepherd. He came so that we might see him and know him. He came to bring life (John 1:4). And his whole ministry was aimed at opening the eyes of all those who would be saved. When one looks at the ministry of Jesus through the lens of a good shepherd, the content of his words and deeds become obvious. The evidence is there if one is willing to look. In fact, the evidence is overwhelming. Jesus displayed all the elements of a good shepherd.

Nonetheless, one might want to challenge Jesus' claim as the Good Shepherd. What is the evidence that singles Jesus out as the Good Shepherd? What sets him apart? How did Jesus demonstrate the traits of a good shepherd? If the evidence is out there, is it compelling enough to warrant a response?

As we saw in the preceding chapter, Jesus was the God of Creation, the God of Genesis, and, therefore, the Messiah. His mere presence in our world demonstrated a shepherd's love and a willingness to reach out to humanity. First, he was willing to descend from heaven to Earth. Second, he was willing to become a part of his own creation. Third, he was willing to become human. In so doing, he had to be willing to shackle his divinity with our humanity. He had to be willing to be touched by all of our human limitations. Fourth, he had to be willing to dwell among us (John 1:14). God actually humbled himself and lived in a world distorted by the sin of man. He who knew no sin entered into a spiritually filthy environment. At every turn, Jesus was confronted with our sin. Nevertheless, he came, and we are fortunate that he did. Without question, "God is totally committed to us" (Frazee, 2015, p. 241).

Jesus was patient, he was kind, he did not envy, he did not boast, and he was not proud. He was not self-seeking, he was not easily angered, and he kept no record of wrong doing (Frazee, 2015, p. 341). Fortunately, for our benefit, a part of his life was recorded in the Gospels. This ancient record contains some of his words and deeds. Through this record, we can begin to see the creative mixture of humanity and divinity (John 1:14). Jesus was willing to become the product of both worlds (Matthew 1:18–25). However, his knowledge and sight were not constantly limited by his humanity. His divine origin and powers continually broke through his humanity. His shepherding skills quite often shatter the darkness of our world; he could not resist touching his sheep with compassion and mercy.

One of the first such events is recorded in John 1:48, when Jesus told Nathanael, "I could see you under the fig tree before Philip found you." As God, Jesus was not subject to the laws of nature. He was the master of all creation, and he could see and hear beyond the limitations of his natural eyes and ears. He was God clothed in our likeness. Yet, he was still one with the Father, and he was still one with the Holy Spirit, and he could see through their eyes and he could hear through their ears (John 17:21). The Good Shepherd's declaration to Nathanael shocked Nathanael because Jesus had not been present earlier when Nathanael and his brother, Philip, met under the fig tree. Yet, Jesus was aware of their meeting and location.

Jesus knew what had been said between the brothers; Jesus was revealing a tiny glimpse of his divinity to Nathanael. This was a microscopic gift, but it was personal, and it had a profound impact upon Nathanael. The event between Nathanael and Philip was unimportant, but it was not overlooked by Jesus. And Jesus took the time to mention it to Nathanael, knowing it would touch Nathanael's heart. Clearly, Jesus was the type of shepherd who did watch over his sheep. Every detail was important to him and his timing and ability to touch the heart was perfect. Nathanael walked away from this encounter knowing that Jesus cared about the tiniest of matters.

The Struggle to Save Judas

One of the very last times Jesus displayed this divine capacity to see and hear far beyond his human limitations can be observed in the betrayal by Judas Iscariot. As the time of Judas' betrayal drew nearer, Jesus began revealing his knowledge of the upcoming event. In fact, during the Last Supper, Jesus openly stated: "one of you will betray me" (Matthew 26:21). This announcement served as a heads-up to the faithful eleven, demonstrating Jesus' awareness of what was unfolding. It was also an act of kindness for the faithful eleven. They would carry these words close to their hearts in the years to come. Jesus knew all about the horror coming toward them and him, and he knew the terrible impact it would have upon his disciples. The faithful eleven did not know how much they needed Jesus' kindness. "Kindness involves doing something deemed positive by the recipient" (Frazee, 2015, p. 435). In addition, the announcement served as a warning to Judas, and the warning also revealed Jesus' compassion for Judas.

In fact, Jesus' love made it imperative for him to warn Judas, and this was not the first time Jesus had warned Judas. It would have been inconceivable for Jesus to remain silent on this most critical night. Judas was about to walk into an eternal nightmare, and Jesus loved him. This warning was an act of benevolence by the Good Shepherd. Goodness can sometimes entail "tough love for the benefit of another because it will genuinely help them" (Frazee, 2015, p. 435).

Obviously, the upcoming intended act of betrayal by Judas would carry a hefty penalty, and Jesus would not allow Judas to walk into this perilous situation without advance warning. Therefore, Jesus stressed the gravity of the act to all twelve disciples through his warning. "But how terrible it will be for my betrayer. Far better for him if he had never been born!" (Matthew 26:24). This announcement shattered the atmosphere;

it must have sounded like an emotional, mental bomb exploding in the room. Its explosion ripped through the tranquility of the evening, stopping everything. Everyone's attention was now focused upon Jesus' night-rendering announcement. The terrible consequences for the upcoming deed struck everyone's ears, including Judas'. The warning was designed to shatter Judas' evil intentions. It was truly "tough love for the benefit of" Judas. It was truly an act of mercy; it was grace extended by the Good Shepherd. The announcement was an act of "absolute Purity, unsullied even by the shadow of sin" (Pink, 2006, p. 51).

Judas' intended evil was confronted by the holiness of God. Judas was being given another opportunity to stop. He did not have to commit this terrible sin. He did not have to follow through with his intended act of betrayal. Judas could choose life for himself and Jesus; he could flee from his intended act. It was not too late. Jesus was offering Judas mercy and grace and forgiveness and love. Jesus was displaying the traits of the Good Shepherd.

Jesus' words did not stand alone. There was the convicting power of the Holy Spirit. Everyone felt the convicting power in the room. "One by one" each of the disciples began to ask Jesus if he were the guilty party (Matthew 26:22). The reality of the warning was permeating the atmosphere; everyone felt its power. Each of the eleven was horrified to think that it could be them, but it was different for Judas. He knew he was the betrayer. Regardless, Judas did not fall down and confess. He did not repent. He remained silent; he remained committed to his course. His whole life was about to be reduced and defined by this one evil act.

In fact, he had already approached the Jewish leadership with the offer to betray Jesus (Matthew 26:14–16). Judas was the one in charge of the betrayal. He was the orchestrator! It was all going according to his plan; he was the one strategizing the perfect time and location for the betrayal (Matthew 26:14–16). Judas was the designer, the architect, the man with the blueprints.

When Jesus' warning pierced the night air, Judas found himself at a crossroad. Would he bow his head, confessing and repenting? Or, would he travel further down the ugly road of deception? Jesus mercifully forced Judas into a crossroad. One way led to life, and the other way led to death. As the Good Shepherd, Jesus would attempt to intervene. Jesus would give Judas a way to escape his intended act of betrayal. Again, it must be noted that Jesus' warning did not stand alone. The Holy Spirit would have been faithful in executing his role. His convicting power would have rained down upon Judas' head (John 16:8). The Holy Spirit would have been playing the tape of Judas' secret discussion with the Sanhedrin; his plot to betray Jesus would have been playing over and over again in his ears.

Unfortunately, Satan had filled Judas to the brim with gall and deception. Judas approached Jesus and said: "Teacher, I'm not the one, am I?" (Matthew 26:25). Did Judas really think he could play the innocent? Did Judas really think that he could place Jesus into some awkward position where Jesus would back down or remain silent? Did he think Jesus could be intimidated? Judas could not blend in with the innocent eleven. He could not hide from the eyes of God. His attempt was pure satanic hypocrisy! "Teacher, I'm not the one, am I?" Yet, how many times have we tried to lie or hide from God. Thankfully, the grace of God is extended to us as well. If you currently stand in God's grace, it was his love and kindness that broke down the barriers of your sin. God once reached out to you and me as he did to Judas.

Once again, Jesus demonstrated his willingness and ability to lead. "And Jesus told him [Judas], 'You have said it yourself'" (Matthew 26:25). Notice Jesus' response to Judas, "You have *said* it yourself" (v. 25). Jesus used the word *said*—past tense. Jesus was intentionally referring to Judas' supposed secret plot with the Sanhedrin. Jesus was referring to what had already been said. What Judas had whispered in secret with the Sanhedrin had been heard by God. Judas could not hide. He could not whisper something into the ears of his coconspirators that God could not hear. None of us can! As we read in Luke 8:17: "For everything that is hidden or secret will eventually be brought to light and made plain to all." Jesus was making it plain to Judas that his whispered secret was known. Surely, you can hear the Holy Spirit replaying the tape once again concerning the plot to betray Jesus. It was being replayed through Judas' memory. He was hearing his own words echoing over and over again in his mind.

Without a doubt, Judas began to waiver, questioning his decision to betray Jesus. Satan had to have noticed this wavering in Judas, leaving Satan with no choice. Satan had to step in and strengthen his man. He could not remain silent and allow Judas to falter (John 13:27). Satan quickly worked against Jesus. Jesus was providing Judas with yet another opportunity to flee from his wicked intentions. Now was not the time for faltering. Judas' evil plot needed to be fortified, braced, girded about in order to nullify Jesus' warning and the Holy Spirit's convicting power. This was something Satan would personally handle. No demon would be sent in to handle this most crucial moment. Satan, himself, would engulf Judas into a sea of pure evil.

Instantly, Judas felt the familiar presence of his master. His former evil intentions were back; there was no more wavering. When Judas next looked at Jesus, Jesus seemed so far away. The power in Jesus' words had diminished, fading into the background. Judas recognized his master's voice. After all, Judas was in the habit of listening to Satan's whisper, but now it was so loud! Judas had stood in the council of evil one too many times. His habit now became fatal; it was too late. Judas could only hear Satan's hissing, and he could only see through Satan's burning eyes. Jesus was not his Lord. Jesus looked so different through Satan's hate-filled eyes. Jesus had been right all along about Judas. Instead of listening to Jesus or the convicting power of the Holy Spirit, Judas would hear his demonic lord, and he would do his lord's bidding.

Obviously, Jesus could see his old adversary in the eyes of Judas; Jesus had looked into those eyes before. Jesus knew Satan when he saw him. Just as the demons could recognize Jesus, Jesus could recognize them. Regrettably, Judas' former resolve to betray Jesus had been strengthened once again. With Judas' resolve to betray firmly in place, Jesus released him to his eternal fate. "Then Jesus told him, 'Hurry. Do it now'" (John 13:27). The sadness in Jesus' tone could not penetrate the overwhelming presence of Satan. Judas had chosen poorly. The convicting power of the Holy Spirit had been rejected. Both Jesus and Satan had intervened during the evening, but Judas' habit of listening to Satan proved fatal. And, if Judas was determined to follow Satan, mercy and grace would be withdrawn. "So Judas left at once, going out into the night" (John 13:30). How poetic! By deliberate choice, Judas went out into the darkness, and the darkness would become his permanent home.

Is it really any different for anyone else? I think not. Jesus, as the Good Shepherd, was willing to speak to anyone willing to listen. Nathanael and Judas are but two examples with extremely different outcomes. Some will be willing to listen, others will not. Regardless, the spiritual provisions needed for life will always be offered to both groups. Jesus provided Nathanael and Judas with a glimpse of his divinity. In fact, Judas was provided with many more glimpses of Jesus' glory over the three years of Jesus' ministry. But it was to no avail. Remember, at first, Nathanael scoffed upon hearing about Jesus (John 1:46). However, Nathanael was open to the truth, and that is where the differences lie between the two men or the two groups.

Nathanael needed only one glimpse of Jesus' supernatural power and his whole life changed. On the other hand, Judas received multiple glimpses. He lived with, traveled with, and ate with the truth, but Judas failed to profit from his time with Jesus. In addition, Judas saw Jesus interacting with thousands upon thousands of people. Judas saw the heart of God, he witnessed the healing power of God, and he saw the mercy and grace of God. Judas also watched some respond correctly to Jesus and he saw some fail to gain from their encounters. Judas had firsthand knowledge and experience with Jesus. There was simply no legitimate excuse for Judas to fail to profit from his interaction with the Son of God. Nevertheless, there is a terrible cost for rejecting the truth—and it will be paid. "The wrath of God is his eternal detestation of all unrighteousness" (Pink, 2006, p. 106).

In the two examples above, Jesus demonstrated his divinity. These were not isolated events; he authenticated his spiritual status as the Good Shepherd hundreds of times. We will explore a few more examples where the glory of the Son of God broke through his humanity, revealing the eternal power of God.

Jesus' First Miracle

The second chapter of the Gospel of John records Jesus' first miracle. In this case, Jesus was attending a wedding, and the wine began to run out. This would have been a social embarrassment for the groom. So, Jesus' mother, Mary, approached Jesus regarding the situation (v. 3). Jesus responded by stating that the problem was not his to solve (v. 4). Nevertheless, Mary instructed the servants to do whatever Jesus told them to do (v. 5). She left the situation in her son's hands. Jesus was free to intervene or not. He immediately looked around and spotted six large water jugs nearby. He ordered the servants to fill them to the brim with water (vs. 6–7). Once the jugs were filled with water, the servants were to draw out some of the water and serve it "to the master of ceremonies" (vs. 7–8).

"When the master of ceremonies tasted the water that was now wine," he was impressed beyond measure (vs. 9–10). He did not know that only moments before, this smooth, properly aged wine had been mere water. The master of ceremonies rated Jesus' wine as the "best" wine of all (v. 10).

At this point, the reader should begin to wonder what divine powers were utilized in the production of this simple yet profound miracle. To answer those questions, one must ask, what are the necessary steps in the natural production of wine? First, a vineyard must be planted and nurtured until it is ready to produce grapes. Second, the vineyard must be made ready for the coming rains. Then, one must wait for the rains which I might add are beyond the power of humans to control (Matthew 5:45). Third, the rain must be absorbed and transported to the developing grapes. Now, additional time is needed for the grapes to mature. This is yet another step in the process that lies beyond the reach of humanity. Fourth, the grapes need to be harvested and transported to the winery for processing. The grape juice must be extracted, and other ingredients added. Again, more time is needed. Fifth, the wine must be properly stored and allowed to age which calls for additional time. Sixth, the wine must be transported to market and purchased. Now, the wine is finally ready to be served and consumed.

Apparently, Jesus saw no reason to pass through all the steps listed above. He did not need a vineyard. He did not need to wait for rains to come. He did not need to wait for the grapes to mature. He did not have to harvest or transport the grapes for processing. He did not have to store the wine, nor did he have to wait for the wine to age. Jesus demonstrated that he was the master of creation and the master of time. He was not dependent upon any natural processes, or upon the labor requirements for harvesting grapes. Remember, in the beginning God created the universe, and it was properly "aged." Our world was perfectly formed, teeming with life. Adam was not formed from the dust of the earth wearing diapers. Adam and Eve were both fully mature adults. The universe was not half-formed, it was fully formed and properly aged. Jesus was the Son of God, and, therefore, he was free and capable of exercising his divine powers. He was the master and the creator of the laws of nature. He was not subject to them. And, according to Sir Thomas Browne, God could step onto the scene at any time and override the laws of nature at will.

> Now this course of Nature God seldom alters or perverts ....Yet this rule of His He doth sometimes pervert, to acquaint the World with His Prerogative, lest the arrogancy [arrogance] of our reason should question His power, and conclude He could not. And thus I call the effects of Nature the works of God. Whose hand and instrument she only is; and therefore to ascribe His actions unto her, is to devolve the honour [honor] of the principal agent upon the instrument .... (McGrath, 2011, p. 98)

His divinity broke through his humanity as he turned water straight into properly aged wine. The master of time and creation was standing in the midst of this wedding feast. Truly, God had been willing to humble himself and become a part of his own creation (Philippians 2:7–11). He was willing to become a man. He was willing to experience hunger like a man, to need sleep like a man, and to experience pain and suffering like a man. He was willing to face rejection like a man, and he was willing to die a horrible death. Jesus was the Good Shepherd. His humanity could not conceal his divinity. His divinity was revealed in spite of his human likeness. Human flesh was simply too weak to conceal the divinity within. Jesus was the manifestation of God. He came as the Good Shepherd in order to show us the way.

Born Again

An additional example of the good attributes of a divine shepherd can be found in the interaction between Nicodemus and Jesus. Nicodemus was a Pharisee and, as such, he was a member of the religious group that stood openly hostile toward

Jesus. Yet, Nicodemus still came to Jesus under the concealment of darkness (John 3:1–2). He could see the presence of God in the miracles performed by Jesus and that was "proof enough" for him (John 3:2). However, openly coming to Jesus could still cause problems for Nicodemus. Nonetheless, Jesus did not hesitate to meet with Nicodemus. The Good Shepherd did not demand perfection from those who came to him, and Jesus could see the hunger in Nicodemus. So, Jesus immediately began to interact with him, explaining how to gain access into the Kingdom of God: "I assure you, unless you are born again, you can never see the Kingdom of God" (John 3:3).

Jesus laid it all out for Nicodemus. Jesus stressed the need to be born again, to believe in him to the point that one's life was totally altered. The believing individual's life was to be centered upon God. This change was to begin with the Holy Spirit giving "new life from heaven" (John 3:3–7). This new life would come from above to anyone willing to surrender. This mystery of being born again is where humanity procures eternal life through the work of Christ Jesus. To be physically born was to enter onto the stage of life. To be born again was to enter onto the stage of eternal life. And Jesus wanted Nicodemus to understand the concept of being born again because it was the only way to "see the Kingdom of God" (v. 3).

Jesus was the Good Shepherd, and he was always ready to provide instruction for those searching for truth. And this was not unusual. God had been speaking to everyone from the beginning of creation. The psalmist wrote:

> The heavens tell of the glory of God. The skies display his marvelous craftsmanship. Day after day they continue to speak; night after night they make him known. They speak without a sound or a word; their voice is silent in the skies; yet their message has gone out to all the earth, and their words to all the world. (Psalm 19:1–4)

God's creation has been speaking to us for hundreds of years. His creative works have been offering instructions year after year, decade after decade, and century after century. In fact, Jonathan Edwards referred to the following instructions from creation as "a kind of voice."

> The works of God are but a kind of voice or language of God to instruct intelligent beings in things pertaining to Himself. And why should we not think that he would teach and instruct by His works in this way.... If we look on these shadows of divine things as the voice of God purposely by them teaching us these and those spiritual and divine things, to show of what excellent advantage it will be, how agreeably and clearly it will tend to convey instruction to our minds, and to impress things on the mind and to affect the mind, by that we may, as it were, have God speaking to us. (McGrath, 2011, p. 103)

Everyone needs to be willing to look and listen for the truth, knowing that God may choose to speak through creation and/or through the Scriptures. In so doing, the results can lead to enlightenment. And, instead of being separated from God and destined for destruction, everyone could become separated from his or her sin through the blood of Christ and united with God. Jesus went on to explain to Nicodemus that this was the whole reason for his coming into the world. He came to save the world not to condemn it (John 3:13–21). As the Good Shepherd, Jesus came to lead the way; he was the gateway into the Kingdom of God (John 10:7). Nicodemus, an active ruling member of the Sanhedrin and a member of a group that was openly hostile toward Jesus, still represented a soul in need of salvation. Accordingly, Jesus was absolutely unwilling to turn him away or anyone away who came searching for truth.

Jesus demonstrated through his interactions with Nicodemus that there would be no prejudiced grouping with God. Each person would be handled and judged by their response to God's offer of salvation (John 3:18). It must be noted again that Nicodemus was a member of a group that was aggressively belligerent toward Jesus, and Nicodemus came at night. He did not want to become a target of his own group's hostilities. Yet, even with all of these negative factors surrounding Nicodemus, Jesus looked beyond the outward appearance. He looked at Nicodemus's heart—nothing else. Therefore, we know that God will judge fairly. Each person will stand or fall before God based upon what they have done with God's offer of life. At the second coming of Jesus, two men could be working in the same field, performing the same or a related task, and still face completely different outcomes. One of them could "be taken, the other left" (Matthew 24:40). In like manner, two women could be grinding flour at the same mill; one could be "taken, the other left" (Matthew 24:41). Each case will be settled on an individual basis. This fact becomes even clearer in the next example.

In Spirit and in Truth

Jesus never focused on the elite while ignoring the lower classes; he was open to everyone. A Samaritan woman who had lost her reputation came under the eye of the Good Shepherd. Jesus was passing through Samaria on his way back to Galilee (John 4:3–4). He was completely worn out, collapsing beside a well to rest (v. 6). It wasn't long before a Samaritan woman came along, and Jesus asked her for a drink (v. 7). The woman was astonished, and she found herself challenging Jesus' motive for speaking with her (v. 9). Jesus casually brushed her challenge to the side and told her that she should be the one asking him for water (v. 10). The woman questioned the source of Jesus' water and Jesus' ability to obtain this offer of "'living water'" (vs. 11–12).

Unquestionably, laden down with more questions than answers, the woman finally asked Jesus for some of his water

(John 4:15). Up to this point, the woman's encounter with Jesus could not have made much sense. Here was this exhausted Jewish stranger sitting beside the well. He started out his conversation with her by asking for water. Then, he jumps from needing water to offering water. Could this man be for real? He had no rope. He had no bucket, and the well was deep. And to top the whole conversation off, Jesus described his water as "a perpetual spring [from] within, giving them [the recipients] eternal life" (John 4:13–14). That had to have sounded weird to the woman. It must have sounded like Jesus may have had a few screws loose.

When was the last time you had a conversation like that with someone? Did you hang in there for long? Probably not—I would guess. Yet, how many of you have questioned God and came away seemingly empty-handed? All of us! At some point or another everyone has encountered this dilemma with God. I have never known God to answer all of my questions to my satisfaction. Better yet, I have never known God to answer half of my questions to my satisfaction. In fact, when I stand and demand an answer I usually get nothing. However, when I get done pitching my little fit due to a lack of answers and start following him again, I usually come upon my answers. I have learned that answers lie down the path of the obedient; we just have to walk a little further than we expected.

God will lead if we are humble enough to follow. That's what this woman was facing with Jesus. He simply did not answer many of her questions. She had to decide who was in the lead, and it was not her. To her credit, she was determined not to allow her unanswered questions to stop her. She was searching for truth, and truth was too important to give up on. She would persist. If this exhausted simple-appearing man could fill in the blanks of life, she wanted to know. Jesus had her undivided attention. This Samaritan woman would follow Jesus' lead and determine later if the results were worth the effort.

Now, the situation gets even more bizarre for the woman. Despite Jesus' failure to answer her previous challenges and questions, Jesus now embarked on a probe into her tragic life while ignoring her request for some of his special water. "'Go and get your husband,' Jesus told her" (John 4:16). Really! The woman's husband had nothing to do with water. Her marital status had nothing to do with their current conversation.

From a natural perspective, the woman had every reason to blow Jesus off, and this was exactly where Jesus wanted her. Jesus hit her with a challenge guaranteed to unearth everything she might want to keep hidden. Her entire life must have flashed before her eyes. This exhausted man with no rope and no bucket was not providing the water he offered. Instead, this man was putting this poor woman on the spot. He was not allowing her to hide her broken, shattered life. Who did Jesus think he was? Her life was none of his business.

Has God ever demanded more from you than you thought he should or could? Was it more than you thought you could bear? If so, you are not the first person to be brought to such a point. The Good Shepherd knows how to lead, but few know how to follow. The woman must have sensed that there was something about this man—something just beyond her ability to see. Could this man lead her from a desolate place into a new life? Her life was broken. She was an outcast. The other women in Samaria didn't even want to associate with her. She lived in a time when a person could not go any lower than where she found herself. She had reached the bottom.

She did not know who Jesus was other than he was a Jew. Socially, he was way above her. He seemed to speak in riddles, but something in his manner touched her thirst for life. Was he promising more than water? She needed water, but she also needed much more. She wanted her search for God answered. She was thirsty for truth. She was thirsty for life, and she did not know where to go to find her answers. Fortunately, she was standing before the Good Shepherd, and Jesus was the source of all her needs (John 14:6).

"'Go and get your husband,' Jesus told her" (John 4:16). What did this demand from this weary stranger have to do with the living water? This stranger's words—what did they mean? The woman thought: *Go get my husband?* How? The woman currently had no husband. In fact, she had five previous husbands, and the man she was currently living with was not her husband (John 4:18). What was she to do? Her personal life had nothing to do with Jesus. All of this stuff was none of the stranger's business. Why was Jesus making this request? Surely this stranger couldn't know her marital history. Did she even need to answer him? Did she need to be honest? Did she need to be truthful? Would he know if she lied? Would it matter if she lied?

Jesus' untimely command was threatening to uncover her entire life. The religious elite would have been quickly offended by Jesus' questions, and they would have stormed off, but not this Samaritan woman. She was searching for life's greatest question. She didn't know that her future hung in the balance at that moment. Her answer would determine the outcome of this exchange between her and God. Jesus was "bringing the woman's sin into the open" (Morris, 1989, p. 264).

One might want to ask: 'What do sin and water have in common?" Well, we might need to ask additional questions like: "Can someone who hides from the truth find truth? Can anyone who lives on a foundation of lies hear truth when it is spoken?" My personal experience says no. Truth is an unknown for the one who hides from truth. Truth is a foreign language to the habitual liar. Truth has the tendency to strip away a person's veneer, and liars do not like that. Their masquerade is more valuable to them than the truth. This Samaritan woman was provided with a choice: She could hide in the darkness or she could step out into the light (John 3:20–21).

The woman spoke the truth; she stepped out into the light: "'I don't have a husband,' the woman replied" (John 4:17). Jesus quickly acknowledged that she had told the truth. "Jesus said, 'You're right. You don't have a husband—for you have had five husbands, and you aren't even married to the man you're living with now'" (John 4:17–18). Once she demonstrated her willingness to be truthful, Jesus explained that it was time for people to worship God in spirit and in truth. He went on to say that God was actively searching for true worshippers who did exactly that—ones who were willing to worship in spirit and in truth (John 4:23–24).

The woman had to meet the Father's requirement of a true worshipper before he would reveal himself. God was not looking for liars. She had to be willing to come to God in spirit and in truth. She was obviously meeting the first requirement of God by searching for God, but there was a second requirement. Fortunately, she was never derailed by Jesus' lack of a direct answer to her spiritual search. In the end, her search for truth, while demonstrating truth, was met with truth—a direct revelation from Jesus. "Then Jesus told her. 'I am the Messiah!'" (John 4:26). The woman's search ended with knowing not only where she could worship, but whom she could worship. She had found God, or better yet, he had found her. He had walked into her life. He met her at the well, and he quenched her thirst.

This Samaritan woman serves as a perfect example of God's willingness to speak, but it is imperative that one has ears to hear. It is also important to note that God will not be dictated to, and he will only be found by those who search for him in spirit and in truth. God will not alter his standards for anyone. I have often wondered how different the conversation might have gone if the Samaritan woman had decided to lie, attempting to hide her marital past. It would have been a terrible personal loss to her, and we would have been potentially robbed of a beautiful insight into the nature of God.

Faith in Jesus

Next, we come to a story of a government official from the city of Capernaum. The man's son was sick and at the point of death (John 4:46–47). The interaction between Jesus and this government official began with the man asking Jesus to come to his home and heal his son. The act of Jesus physically coming to his home was in fact a request for a physical sign aimed at sustaining the man's belief that all would be well. He thought he needed Jesus to travel with him. The idea was that Jesus, the healer, was coming to the rescue. No doubt Jesus realized the doubts assaulting the man's mind, hence, the need for encouragement—a sign. But Jesus knew that the man's faith could sustain him without a tangible sign. Obviously, the man had already demonstrated his ability to believe in Jesus by traveling to meet Jesus. He traveled toward Jesus without any assistance from a sign, and, in reality, he could travel back without one.

Therefore, Jesus would work to separate the man from his supposed need for a sign. Jesus' plan was simple; he would set the man free from this mental stumbling block. So, "Jesus asked, 'Must I do miraculous signs and wonders before you people will believe in me?'" (John 4:48). Jesus was asking the man if his faith was anchored in signs and wonders or in him as Lord. What was the object of the man's faith? Was it in signs and wonders or in Jesus? The man needed to answer this question. Jesus was forcing the man to realize where his faith rested, and it was not in a sign or in a wonder. Jesus, himself, was the source of the man's faith—the man just needed to realize it. The man just needed a little help, a little nudge. His faith was right there, waiting to emerge. Jesus knew he could send the man home—alone. "Then Jesus told him, 'Go back home. Your son will live!' And the man believed Jesus' word and started home" (John 4:50). The response was immediate. The man's faith made his ears ready to hear, and he was quick to respond.

The man was no longer paralyzed or frozen by the need for a sign; he was free to travel home, but he was not going home empty-handed. He was holding onto the words of his Lord. Jesus had lit a little fire to kindle his faith, and the man's faith had the power to hold onto what he could not see. He knew his son would live, whereas before, his son was dying. Jesus had supercharged this man's faith and "such a person does not need supplementary arguments or evidence in order to know and to know with confidence that he is in fact experiencing the Spirit of God" (Craig, 2008, p. 43). This walk home would be different; it was full of expectancy. The government official believed the word spoken. The Good Shepherd had shown the man his way home.

> While he [the government official] was on his way, some of his servants met him with the news that his son was alive and well. He asked them when the boy had begun to feel better, and they replied, 'Yesterday afternoon at one o'clock his fever suddenly disappeared!' Then the father realized it was the same time that Jesus had told him, 'Your son will live.' And the officer and his entire household believed in Jesus. (John 4:51–53)

Now, Jesus turned his attention toward the crowd that was following him. He had fed many of them the day before, and they pursued him across the Sea of Galilee. Upon their arrival, they wanted to know how he had crossed the sea. Jesus casually brushed aside their questioning much like he did with the Samaritan woman's questions, and he began speaking directly toward their need. Jesus informed them that they were pursuing him for all the wrong reasons, "you want to be with me because I fed you . . . you shouldn't be so concerned about perishable things like food. Spend your energy seeking the eternal life that I, Son of Man, can give you" (John 6:26–27). In other words,

I Am the Good Shepherd

Jesus was more than a source of food. Their expectations were much too low. They wanted Jesus for all the wrong reasons.

Jesus presented the same requirements to this crowd as he had to the Samaritan woman. Anyone who seeks after God must come in spirit and in truth (John 4:23–24). The Samaritan woman had originally come to the well seeking natural water. During her journey with Jesus, she allowed Jesus to shift her search into the spiritual realm. In fact, Jesus forcefully, but gently, insisted that she add truth to her search. The Samaritan woman allowed Jesus to lead her into the Kingdom of God, but this crowd stubbornly refused to follow Jesus' lead. They knew what they wanted, and they would not be deterred.

They came with their eyes glued on the temporal—food. In so doing, they turned the miracles of Jesus into a means or a goal in and of themselves. They failed to allow the miracles to pull their eyes upward. Instead, they pulled the miracles of God down into their domain, reducing the miracles to no more than a source of free food. What an insult to the power of God. Jesus was performing miracles to announce the nearness of the Kingdom of God, not the nearness of a quick, cheap meal. Jesus had more to offer, and the crowd needed more. The crowd did not meet the basic requirements of either spirit or truth. The crowd could not make it on bread alone (Matthew 4:4). When a person or a group, like this crowd, resists God, "it is never just because of lack of evidence or because of intellectual difficulties: at root, he refuses to come because he willingly ignores and rejects the drawing of God's Spirit on his heart" (Craig, 2008, p. 47).

This incorrect attitude, if left unchallenged, would leave the crowd in control, and they were not the shepherds. Jesus was! Plus, if their goals remained, Jesus would have been reduced to a means to an end. And miracles were not the end-game. Jesus was! The purpose of miracles was to point people toward God. The spiritual significance of the miracles was beyond their comprehension. That is why Jesus said, "you shouldn't be so concerned about perishable things like food. Spend your energy seeking the eternal life that I, Son of Man, can give you" (John 6:26–27). The crowd's thinking was on the here and now. They were of the Earth, and they were trying to figure out how best they could use Jesus for their own means. There was a complete conflict between Jesus and the crowd. The crowd could not see beyond their own goal. So, the crowd "replied, 'What does God want us to do?'" (John 6:28).

"Jesus told them, 'This is what God wants you to do: Believe in the one he has sent'" (John 6:29). Jesus' instructions were simple. God wanted them to believe in the Son for their eternal needs. In other words, there was much more to Jesus than a free meal. They needed to adjust their search from the physical into the spiritual, if they truly wanted to find something that would last. With their present method of searching, they would never find eternal life. The Good Shepherd was trying to lead them into greener pastures. The crowd needed to stop pursuing after that which would perish. Food, like their physical body, would pass away, but those who grab onto the Son would never die (John 6:40).

Without a doubt, the crowd understood what Jesus was saying, but they still wanted to dictate the terms. Look at their response: "They replied, 'You must show us a miraculous sign if you want us to believe in you. What will you do for us?'" (John 6:30). Did you catch the problem and the pattern? The crowd was following Jesus because of his miraculous ability to provide food. They had seen and experienced Jesus' unusual power. The crowd demonstrated that they understood the term "one sent" was a direct reference to Jesus himself, but that understanding did not alter their position. The crowd still wanted to be in control. "What will you do for us?" Really!?

Do you realize that their demand placed Jesus in a subordinate role? The crowd wanted the lead; Jesus needed to meet their expectations. "What will you do for us?" Their stubbornness stood in stark contrast to Jesus' complete willingness to follow the leading of his Father. The crowd was not teachable, but the Samaritan woman was. She was willing to be led. This crowd had gained nothing but a full stomach—a temporary reprieve from hunger. It would not sustain them. In contrast, the Samaritan woman had gained everything from her encounter with Jesus. In the end, everyone determines how much or how little they receive from God, and the amount they receive is directly connected to their willingness to submit to God. Those with stubborn hearts receive little to nothing from God, but the humble receive in abundance (Psalm 25:9-14).

Salvation Is on God's Terms

In like manner, the Sanhedrin made the same spiritual mistake as the crowd; they failed and/or refused to evaluate the spiritual evidence that occurred during their interaction with Jesus. This failure of the Sanhedrin is recorded in the seventh chapter of the Gospel of John. The Festival of Shelter had arrived, and "midway through the festival, Jesus went up to the Temple and began to teach. The Jewish leaders were surprised when they heard him. 'How does he know so much when he hasn't studied everything we've studied?' they asked" (John 7:14-15).

Without question the Jewish leaders recognized the spiritual wisdom in the teachings of Jesus. They knew this was highly unusual. In fact, it was staggering. Without formal training, Jesus was in possession of a vast amount of spiritual wisdom. Nevertheless, the Jewish leadership wanted Jesus dead (John 7:1). They were actively searching for him during the festival (John 7:11). When they found him, they were overwhelmed by his wisdom, rendering them motionless. Despite their disapproval of him, Jesus' godly wisdom penetrated their stubborn hearts. This was the perfect response; their powerlessness before Jesus was their spiritual cue to stop and reevaluate their intended course of action. This was the spiritual evidence they needed. This was their gift from God the Father, and this was God's stamp of approval upon his Son. Undoubtedly, this was also God's direct challenge to them.

At last, the Jewish leadership had come to the right question. Where did Jesus get all this heart-tugging wisdom? Did it materialize out of thin air? What does one do when one is confronted by the supernatural? They were encountering a deep-seated wisdom coming from someone who had no apparent training. So, if the wisdom was there, and there was no apparent training, what was the only remaining conclusion? Jesus had to have been trained by an unknown source. So, what was the next most logical step in identifying the source of the training? Simple! Identify the type of wisdom being exhibited. Once one has identified the type of wisdom being exhibited, one has identified the source.

And it needs to be remembered that the Jewish leadership was spellbound by the spiritual wisdom exhibited by Jesus. Jesus was not spouting off head knowledge, he was demonstrating a functioning, applicable, working knowledge of spiritual matters. This was not a demonstration of "book" learning. Jesus was functioning on a totally different level from the Pharisees. Jesus' wisdom was smashing the Jewish leadership's monopoly on book learning. Yet, with all of their book learning, no one was profiting from it, including them. Jesus surpassed their understanding. His authority exceeded theirs (Matthew 7:29). Jesus' understanding was tangible, it was applicable, and it was alive. The Pharisees were touched by it. This was the spiritual evidence they needed. They were staring truth in the eyes. They were looking into the eyes of God.

The Jewish leadership was being called by God to humble themselves before Jesus; they were obligated to bend their knees and bow their heads, but they refused. Their open hostilities should have stopped. After all, if Jesus' wisdom had been corrupt, they would have been free and obligated to renounce his teachings and point out his error. But, instead of attacking the functioning, breathing wisdom of Jesus, they attacked Jesus and, thereby, they stood condemned. They were rejecting the Good Shepherd who was presenting the wisdom of God.

Furthermore, this was not the only spiritual evidence available for examination. They also had available to them many powerful miracles. They had Old Testament passages being fulfilled by Jesus, and those same passages bore witness to the identity of Jesus. In addition, they had Jesus' godly conduct. He never got nasty with them; he never berated people. He had countless acts of kindness and grace. All of this evidence should have been added into the mix.

What was the source of the miracles? Did the miracles conflict with the Scriptures? Did the conduct of Jesus conflict with the Scriptures? Did Jesus' wisdom conflict with the Scriptures? Again, the answer to all of these questions was a resounding no. The lifestyle, the miracles, and the wisdom of Jesus all pointed to the same unavoidable conclusion. The spiritual evidence for Jesus was overwhelming if one looked at it from a logical viewpoint. There was no corrupt lifestyle on the part of Jesus. False miracles could have been uncovered, and faulty wisdom could have been challenged and publicly denounced.

The Jewish leaders had but two options if they could not crush the wisdom, the miracles, and the conduct of Jesus. They could accept Jesus as the one sent by God, or they could reject him. They were left with no middle ground, and that appears to be the way God deals with humankind. There is simply no middle ground with God. You either believe in Christ, or you reject him. Salvation is offered and accepted on God's terms, or not at all. Humanity will never find salvation on its terms. God will be the one to set the standard, and humanity will comply or die. There is really no debate. Accept God's terms or reject God's terms. As the Good Shepherd, Jesus offered sound guidance to the Jewish leadership; they were provided with the terms of salvation.

The Redemptive Work of Christ

"I am the good shepherd. The good shepherd lays down his life for the sheep" (John 10:11). Jesus was constantly placing his life in danger every time he presented God's message of life. He came to seek and to save that which was lost (Luke 19:10). He came to bring the light of God into a dark world (John 1:4–5). He came to save, not to condemn (John 3:17).

"I am the good shepherd; I know my own sheep, and they know me, just as my Father knows me and I know the Father. And I lay down my life for the sheep" (John 10:14–15). Jesus never flinched from facing the wolves. He spoke the truth, knowing that his death was quickly approaching. He came to lay down his life, knowing that, when he was raised from the dead, he would bring with him all those who believed in him. He came to die that we who believe might live. Without his death there would be no life, but for all who believes in him, they have passed from death into life (John 2:24).

"The Father loves me because I lay down my life that I may have it back again. No one can take my life from me. I lay down my life voluntarily" (John 10:17–18). In just a few words, Jesus revealed the love relationship that existed between God the Father and God the Son. Jesus came to take away the sin of humankind, removing the separation between humanity and God (John 1:29). For all who accept the redemptive work of Christ, they have "become the children of God" (John 1:12). All believers experience a new birth through the love of God (John 1:13). Our heavenly experience will be full of awe and wonder; heaven will not be boring because God is not boring (Alcorn, 2004, p. 410).

Look at creation! Our world is full of beauty and diversity. There is nothing boring about what God has created. "Sin doesn't make life interesting; it makes life empty. Sin doesn't create adventure; it blunts it. Sin doesn't expand life; it shrinks it. Sin's emptiness inevitably leads to boredom" (Alcorn, 2004, p. 410).

So many people today are chasing after success, but what is success? No matter how many possessions we may acquire, no matter how many promotions we may obtain, no matter how much recognition we may accumulate, what does all that profit us in the end? We all die. Everyone leaves everything behind. "God never calls us to be successful. He calls us to be faithful" (Frazee, 2015, p. 460). From a worldly viewpoint Jesus had nothing (Matthew 8:20). Yet, it was Jesus who could offer eternal life to everyone who would believe in him (John 3:16).

> If there is no God, then man and the universe are doomed. Like prisoners condemned to death, we await our unavoidable execution. There is no God, and there is no immortality. And what is the consequence of this? It means that life itself is absurd. (Craig, 2008, p. 72)

When Jesus came as the Good Shepherd, he came to confront the wolves of humanity's own imagination. Humanity and the universe are not doomed. The only thing doomed is sin and evil; they will come to an end. Jesus came to assure us that there is a God; he wanted us to know that he holds immortality in his hands. Therefore, he opened his hands; he shed his blood that we might live. In God, there is no absurdity.

Jesus was and will remain forever the Good Shepherd, the one who laid down his life that others might have eternal life through his blood. He brought good gifts to us, and he repeatedly demonstrated his qualities as the Good Shepherd.

CHAPTER 3

I Am the Resurrection

(John 11)

THE GOAL OF THE eleventh chapter of the Gospel of John was to introduce Jesus as the fulfillment of the resurrection. After all, Jesus clearly stated to Martha: "I am the resurrection and the life" (John 11:25). The resurrection story is centered on a tight-knit family structure that consisted of Mary, Martha, and their brother, Lazarus. All three family members were personal friends of Jesus, and he loved each one. They were of great importance to him, and his interaction with each one was incredibly unique. The resurrection of Lazarus took place in Judea. In fact,

> [T]he raising of Lazarus from death to life is seen to be the event which led the Jewish authorities to take decisive action against Jesus; and it is also the 'sign' which discloses more clearly than any other the meaning of His death and resurrection. (Tasker, 1960, p. 137)

Martha and Mary's response to Jesus was completely different, and it will take a deliberate effort to ferret out the dissimilarities that are hidden treasures and spiritual insights that must not be overlooked. The sisters' different levels of comprehending the resurrection power within Jesus resulted in drastically different interactions with Jesus. However, if we dare to examine the sisters' every movement, we can gain an extremely enlightening perception of God's spiritual realm. It is my hope that you will allow yourself the necessary time to acquire an understanding in line with the original intended message of chapter eleven.

> A man named Lazarus was sick. He lived in Bethany with his sisters, Mary and Martha. This is the Mary who poured the expensive perfume on the Lord's feet and wiped them with her hair. Her brother, Lazarus was sick. So the two sisters sent a message to Jesus telling him, "Lord, the one you love is very sick." (John 11:1–3)

The story begins by allowing the reader to know that Lazarus was seriously sick; in fact, he was deathly sick. In desperation, the sisters turned to Jesus, hoping for a miracle that would stay the hand of death. The urgency of the situation compelled the sisters to act with speed and diligence. A messenger was sent with a strong, clear, unmistakable message of life and death. There was no time for error. Therefore, Mary and Martha would have sent a messenger with enough intelligence to properly convey the urgency of the situation. After all, their brother's life hung in the balance. We can assume that the message was clear and that the messenger accomplished his task.

So, their plea safely reached Jesus. And the sisters likely assumed that everything would be all right. Jesus would come quickly, and their brother, Lazarus, would not die. Right! Well, not exactly. God's timing was different from that of the sisters, and that should not be surprising to us. God's timing in answering prayers and his method of answering prayers have not changed. God does not operate according to our way of thinking, or according to our time frame. And he surely did not operate in the way Mary and Martha thought he would.

But, Mary and Martha were believers in Jesus, and on top of that they were Jesus' personal friends. It seems like they should have had an inside edge with Jesus. After all, they ate with Jesus, they spoke with Jesus, and they no doubt laughed with him. Yet, Jesus did not do as they thought he should. Mary and Martha thought their circumstances were powerful enough and serious enough to dictate Jesus' schedule. Wrong! Their circumstances were not any different from what we face today. We can and do encounter sickness and death just like Mary and Martha.

In addition, modern-day Christians are also the friends of Jesus (John 15:14–15). We set our petitions before God just like Mary and Martha. We hope our expectations and prayers will be answered as well. Then, we, like the sisters, wait for an answer. And we, like the sisters, do not always get the answers we want. When we turn to Jesus, we need to remember that we are dealing with an eternal God. And according to Isaiah 55:9, God's thoughts are higher than our thoughts. God has a different perspective. His perspective is eternal; ours is temporal. This fact held true in Jesus' day as well. Jesus did not think on a temporal plane. His thoughts were focused on the Father's agenda—not ours. Therefore, the request of Mary and Martha would not be answered—at least, not in the way they thought it should be. In fact, their request actually set the stage for a temporary conflict between them and their Lord.

It is critical to note that, at this point, the goal of Mary and Martha was to preserve the life of Lazarus, and this goal stood in direct opposition to the end goal of Jesus. That's right! You read the previous statement correctly. The goal driving Mary and Martha stood in complete opposition to God's plan, and Jesus would follow God's plan. The sisters wanted Jesus to move quickly before death had the opportunity to speak, but that was simply not in God's immediate plan. On the contrary, Jesus would allow death to speak, and then and only then would he make his move. And, of course, when Jesus did make his move and when he did speak, his words would be remembered. Jesus would openly display his resurrection power. All would be invited to see the raising of Lazarus as the prelude to the holiness God would be one day displaying at the cross (Pink, 1975, p. 54).

Please think as we continue through this chapter. This entire eleventh chapter of John, this entire story, was devoted to the concept of the resurrection, but there was more to be understood. Yes. There would be a resurrection in the last days. Nevertheless, God did not want anyone to overlook the fact that Jesus was the personification of the resurrection. The resurrection power was present in bodily form, dwelling among men. And Jesus would demonstrate this reality through Lazarus' immediate resurrection. The resurrection power of God needed to be seen, it needed to be heard, and it needed to be experienced. The words and the message of Jesus were life. Those who heard and received the words of Jesus would rise with him into a newness of life; everyone else would perish.

In addition, there was a subordinate concept hidden within this event as well. Just as Mary and Martha's expectations or pleas could not influence the unfolding of their brother's resurrection, neither will God allow your expectations or demands to play a part in the final resurrection. Everything will proceed exactly as God has planned. No one will have the power to alter the resurrection to come. However, by the grace of God, all can approach the coming resurrection with confidence based upon the work of Christ.

And, of course, Jesus could not produce a demonstration of the coming resurrection without a death. Therefore, Lazarus, a friend of Jesus, was going to die. No death equals no demonstration of a resurrection. Again, Jesus could not resurrect Lazarus unless Lazarus first died. The concept of a resurrection requires both a death and the raising of a life. After Lazarus was resurrected, he resumed his fellowship with Jesus. It will be the same for every believer. Remember, death cannot separate us from the love of God (Romans 8:38).

Mary and Martha's momentary loss and their momentary grief would pass just like yours and mine. Jesus came to do the will of his Father, and it was the Father's will for Mary, Martha, the disciples, and all future Christians to understand that Jesus, the Son of God, was the resurrection. God was placing great importance upon this event. Lazarus would die. Mary and Martha would be plunged into grief, but their loss and their grief would give way to a greater joy. The costs would be high, but the gains were to be even higher. God would do that which was right as he continues to do today. God still does not always answer in the way we would like him to or within our time frame, and that has not changed! We, like Mary and Martha, will see the glory of God in due time. For now, it is our time to trust, to wait, and to expectantly watch for the hand of God.

Death is real. Everyone who is ever born will die, but not everyone who experiences death will be held captive by death. And that is the whole point of the resurrection story. What will happen at your death? Will it mark the beginning of your end? Will it mark the beginning of an eternal state of agony and torment? The rich man in Luke 16:19–31 regretted his final resting place; he cried out in anguish and regret. On the other hand, death can be the last enemy to be conquered (1 Corinthians 15:26). The issue of the resurrection is looming before everyone—no one will be able to avoid their rendezvous with death. The issue of eternity needs to be addressed before it is too late. The resurrection issue was important enough that the Holy Spirit orchestrated this entire event of Lazarus' death and resurrection. The cost born by Mary, Martha, and Lazarus were set aside. Their pain was exchanged for our potential gain.

Please do not neglect so great a gift (Romans 6:23). After all, a time of accounting is quickly approaching.

The Prophecy

Now, we come to the words of Jesus. We encounter Jesus' response to Mary and Martha's plea for help. "Lazarus' sickness will not end in death. No, it is for the glory of God. I, the Son of God, will receive glory from this" (v. 4). Jesus' reply was most likely not even remotely understood by Mary and Martha. They may have taken Jesus' words to mean that he would prevent Lazarus' death in that he would arrive in time to save his friend's life. In fact, I would venture to guess that most Christians today fail to understand Jesus' response unless they are reminded that Jesus came as a priest, as a king, and as a prophet.

Obviously, there may have been times when Jesus spoke as a priest. There may have been times when he spoke strictly as a king, and other times when he spoke as a prophet. In light of these facts, the question we might want to ask right now is: "Was Jesus speaking from one of these particular positions on this particular day?" And the answer is definitely yes! Jesus' statement above was a prophecy. His prophecy accurately outlined the entire account before one step of it was ever taken. And, without a doubt, his prophecy was dead accurate. Let's take a few moments and examine the veracity of his prophecy.

In verse 4, we read: "Lazarus' sickness will not end in death." First, it needs to be stated that all prophecies need to be taken in their entirety. In other words, a prophecy cannot be fully understood or appreciated until all of its components have come to pass. Obviously, the first part of Jesus' prophecy should not be isolated from the rest of the prophecy. The story of Lazarus does not end with him being dead. In fact, the story only starts out with sickness and death. Then the story transitions into Lazarus' resurrection.

I Am the Resurrection

Needless to say, Jesus' prophecy never stated that Lazarus would not die; it never claimed that death would not occur. He simply claimed that death would not have the final word. Jesus knew his friend would die, but Jesus also knew that he would demonstrate the reality of the resurrection to come when he raised Lazarus from the dead. The prophecy was never about death; it was about life. It was about the resurrection to come. As the author Pink points out, "power is that which gives life and action to all the perfections of the Divine nature" (1975, p. 58).

Death could not keep Lazarus in the grave. Jesus' power could reach into and beyond the grave. He was not concerned about death being allowed to speak—first. He did not fear death. Jesus was life; he was the essence of life. Death was powerless next to him, and Jesus wanted Mary and Martha and all believers to understand this divine reality. Everyone needs to embrace Jesus' eternal perspective. Mary and Martha may have feared the power of death, but not Jesus! He could speak after death spoke, and it would be his words that would ring throughout eternity. Death would fall silent.

Now, let's move on into the second portion of Jesus' prophecy and take the necessary time to examine its significance: "No, it is for the glory of God" (v. 4). The middle portion of Jesus' prophecy has everything to do with the placement of glory. The glory in this resurrection story would not be retained by death. Death would be stripped of its finality. It would be stripped of its sting, and it would be stripped of its glory. The glory would be transferred to God the Father where it rightfully belonged.

In fact, the theme of Jesus' whole prophecy was all about the proper, legitimate placement of glory. As we travel through this resurrection event, you will see death being glorified multiple times, and this was an affront to God. You will also see Jesus' negative reaction toward this improper glorification of death. Death normally had the final say or so it appeared; but, in this case, death would have its weakness exposed.

We need to remember that God does not receive glory from sickness or death, and God does not receive the right glorification due his name when an individual's vision of God's greatness is less than what it should be. If an individual's vision of God is diminished by the seeming largeness of death that is a major offense to God. In fact, any display of indignity toward God is the product of unbelief or a gross lack of faith in God. Either way, God frowns upon sharing his glory or upon receiving a diminished glory.

Therefore, as we travel though the eleventh chapter of the Gospel of John you will notice just how many times death—not God—was being glorified. This improper glorification of death needed to be stopped, but, it would not be stopped until Jesus personally stripped away the sting and the finality of death which leads us directly into the third and final part of Jesus' prophecy: "I, the Son of God, will receive glory from this" (v. 4).

The glory of the Son of God can be seen through his prophecy as it unfolds. Jesus outlined all of the events, both verbal and nonverbal, before any of them occurred. He knew the beginning as well as the end. He was cognizant of his role and what he would be teaching. He knew each person's level of faith and how much growth they would encounter. Jesus was also painfully aware of how large death was in the eyes of his disciples, and in the eyes of Mary and Martha. He could see their approaching struggles, their pain, and their sorrows, but he also knew that he would shatter all of their misconceptions. Death would not be glorified in the end. This sickness would not end in death's glorification. Jesus was bringing a fresh new vision of God, and this new vision of God would shatter the grip of death. All the glory would be transferred to God through the actions of the Son.

Once again, notice the wording of Jesus' prophecy. Watch for the improper placement of glory and how it was transferred. If Jesus' prophecy is accurate, the reader should first see different individuals glorifying death. And, of course, this was a spiritual error that was in the process of being corrected and, once Jesus reduced the size and the finality of death, the participants would start directing all their adoration toward God.

I would like to paraphrase and expand on Jesus' prophecy for clarification purposes as we get started. [At first, death would be seen as large. In fact, it would be larger than God and larger than the Son of God. As a result, Mary and Martha would want the Son of God to come quickly before death had a chance to speak because once death spoke it would be too late. However, the Son of God would allow death to speak, and then the Son of God would crush death and its false finality. Death had no power before God, and God would not share his glory with anyone or anything. Once the Son of God crushed death, then everyone would glorify the Father. Jesus would have opened their eyes, decreasing the sting of death. As will be demonstrated, until Jesus completed his work, the glory due God would be given elsewhere. Jesus' actions would right this terrible wrong.]

I Will Go and Wake Him

Now, it is time to begin our journey, allowing Jesus' prophecy to guide our footsteps. His prophecy should be allowed to function as the lens that enables us to focus in on the important aspects of the story. We must learn from the master, recognizing his guiding hand. The Gospel account tells us: "Although Jesus loved Martha, Mary, and Lazarus, he stayed where he was for the next two days and did not go to them" (v. 5). However, Jesus was not idly standing by; the stage was being set. He was acutely aware of the passage of time. The wait was part of God's plan. Jesus simply needed to wait for two more days before he began his journey to meet with Martha and Mary.

Did you notice in verse five, as the story began to unfold, the Holy Spirit mentioned Martha first? Interesting! Why? Was that a hint? Was there a particular order? Remember, in the beginning of the chapter, Mary was mentioned first followed by a brief introduction of her. But then, following Jesus' prophecy and the beginning of the actual story, Martha is mentioned first. Are we seeing an order of prominence beginning to emerge? After Jesus waited two more days, he turned to his disciples and said, "Let's go to Judea again" (v. 7).

The disciples responded with absolute disbelief. Are you crazy? Are you for real? They said, "Teacher, only a few days ago the Jewish leaders in Judea were trying to kill you. Are you going there again?" (v. 8). The disciples could not believe their ears. Jesus had to be mistaken, or they must have misheard him. Why would Jesus "venture into the lion's" den again (Bruce, 1983, p. 241)? Surely, Jesus was not suggesting that he intended to go back into an area where his life had already been threatened. Notice that Jesus didn't even address their concerns for his safety. He was on another playing field all together. His life could not be taken from him. He would lay it down when the time was right (John 10:18). Jesus never lost his focus, and he responded to his disciples' astonishment with the following statement: "Our friend Lazarus has fallen asleep, but now I will go and wake him up" (v. 11).

Jesus needed to update his disciples regarding Lazarus' status. Lazarus was dead, and Jesus informed his disciples that he would rectify the situation when he got there. According to Jesus, Lazarus' current status was not permanent. Lazarus would be resurrected because Jesus would "go and wake him up" (v. 11). There are a few interesting things that need to be pointed out here. First, Jesus did not need anyone to keep him a-breast of the situation. He knew how the events were unfolding. Second, the word Jesus used to update his disciples regarding Lazarus' death was a word that could be used to convey the idea of sleep or death. The meaning of the word Jesus used would normally be determined by the context in which it was given.

I Am the Resurrection

This word usage by Jesus provides valuable insights into his mind. Just as you and I can go into the next room and awaken someone out of sleep, Jesus could go into the next room and awaken someone out of death. For Jesus, death was just as powerless before him as sleep is before you, or me. Death was a small thing to our Lord. He was not standing in awe of death. Third, Jesus plainly told the disciple that he would awaken Lazarus upon his arrival, and he did not stutter. His words were not a faint little whisper in the form of a hope. Jesus clearly stated his position and his intended actions. He would "go and wake him up" (v. 11). This should have been plain enough.

> The disciples said, "Lord, if he is sleeping, that means he is getting better!" They thought Jesus meant Lazarus was having a good night's rest, but Jesus meant Lazarus had died. Then he told them plainly, "Lazarus is dead . . . ." (John 11: 12–14)

Once again, there are several interesting things to consider in this passage. First, the disciples took Jesus' words to mean that Lazarus was sleeping. To them, this was an encouraging update on Lazarus. Earlier, the news about Lazarus had been critical. Now, they assumed that Jesus was letting them know that Lazarus was sleeping peacefully after a near-death experience. What a relief they must have felt. Lazarus, their friend, would recover. Second, the disciples did not already have an updated account of Lazarus' status. The update Jesus had given them was a news flash. Third, Jesus knew about Lazarus' condition; he was not dependent on human messengers. Fourth, Jesus knew that Lazarus would not recover without some kind of intervention. And fifth, Jesus corrected their misunderstanding and openly stated for clarification purposes that Lazarus was dead. There would be no normal physical recovery as the disciples first imagined.

However, based upon the information Jesus had just given the disciples, there should have been an outburst of joy and excitement. Lazarus was dead, but Jesus was going to awaken him from death. If they had listened to Jesus' words, no one would have wanted to miss out on this trip. In fact, there should have been a race to see who could get there first to watch Lazarus being raised from the dead. What a gift! They were about to watch Jesus raise Lazarus right before their eyes, but no one cried out with excitement.

On the contrary, the mood of the disciples was pathetic at best. "Thomas, nicknamed the Twin, said to his fellow disciples, 'Let's go too—and die with Jesus'" (v. 16). What? What just happened? Where did all the excitement and joy go? Lazarus was about to be raised from the dead. Why the gloomy mood? Lazarus' tomb was about to be empty. Jesus was going to conquer death by raising his friend. Death was about to be swallowed up (1 Corinthians 15:55).

The glory and the excitement that should have enveloped the entire setting were missing. Instead of glorifying God for what was about to happen, homage was being paid to death. Death was being glorified. According to the disciples, death had spoken; O mighty death thou are an immovable god. You have swallowed our friend, and now, Jesus acts like he wants to be killed too. Therefore, we should all go and die. After all, no one can avoid you. O death, no one can stand before your mighty power. Not even Jesus! Hey! Something has gone terribly wrong.

Wait just a minute! What happened to the words of Jesus? Did they simply disappear? Were they spoken? The Scriptures record Jesus as having said, "but now I will go and wake him up" (v. 11). Jesus spoke about being awakened. There were no words of death in Jesus' statement. There was nothing but triumph in his words, but there was nothing but defeat coming out of the mouth of the disciples. Their words and actions glorified death just like Jesus' prophecy foretold. This misplaced reverence for the power of death must have deeply grieved Jesus. It was, if nothing else, a major slap in his face.

In essence, Thomas and the other disciples saw death as greater than the Son of God. If Jesus was about to die, Thomas had "no wish to survive him" (Bruce, 1983, p. 242). The enormity of death stole the very words Jesus had just spoken. Glory was enveloping the setting, but it was not a glorification of God. Please notice that Jesus didn't even gift the disciples with any further discussion. No words came to encourage their faith. Why would Jesus speak any further? They already failed to hear his words. In fact, his words of life had no impact upon them. His words of life should have established a mood of expectation and excitement, but they hadn't. More words from Jesus would have been a waste of his time. The disciples had not retained, nor could they recall his words: "I will go and wake him up" (v. 11). How sad! The disciples could only hear the echoing of the word *dead*. And the word *dead* gave birth to their spiritually negative behavior, closing the mouth of their Savior. They effectively silenced Jesus with their unbelief. Unbelief is destructive. It can clearly hinder one's ability to hear.

Finally, Jesus arrived near the village of Bethany. When Martha learned that Jesus was coming, she went to meet him, but Mary did not go with her (v. 20). The difference between the sisters starts becoming obvious from this point onward. Martha heard that Jesus was coming, and she immediately went out to meet him. That was not the case for Mary; she did not go out to meet Jesus. Why? Did she not hear about Jesus' arrival? That could be possible, but it is doubtful. Why do the Scriptures point out that she stayed in the house (v. 20)? If she didn't know about Jesus' arrival, she wouldn't have known to go meet him, and there would not have been any need to record the fact that she stayed behind. Nevertheless, we need to be fair. So, at this point, we don't need to draw any conclusions. That can wait until later.

The story continues with a dialogue between Martha and Jesus. "Martha said to Jesus, 'Lord, if you had been here, my brother would not have died. But even now I know that God will give you whatever you ask'" (vs. 21–22). You may want to notice that the Bible records Martha as the only one Jesus actually carried on a dialogue with to any lengthy degree. In addition, she remained standing, and she expressed her faith in Jesus even in this dark hour. Martha was a woman to be admired. She expressed her pain and suffering by blaming Jesus. "Lord, if you had been here, my brother would not have died" (v. 21). Gracefully, Jesus did not berate her for this statement. After all, he could have come sooner and prevented the death of Lazarus. In fact, Jesus could also have prevented the death of Lazarus from a distance.

However, Martha did not stop with just an accusation. She also spoke words of faith; she still believed in her Lord. "But even now I know that God will give you whatever you ask" (v. 22). Not even the loss of her brother could crush her faith. She believed in Jesus. Surrounded, enveloped, and encased in grief, Martha's faith refused to die. Her heart knew what her mind could not grasp. She would believe in Jesus. He was the Lord of her heart, and her heart called out to him—"even now I know that God will give you whatever you ask" (v. 22).

Martha's faith, though battered and bruised, could still motivate her ability to hope. She spoke words of faith. Her hope was bursting through all her pain; she could still glorify Jesus. Her heart still clung to the belief that Jesus was greater than the circumstance gripping her. "But even now I know that God will give you whatever you ask" (v. 22). It was this spark of faith that Jesus chose to address. Jesus knew that the rest of her words were the product of pain and loss. And, of course, pain and loss are born out of circumstances, and circumstances are subject to the power of God. Martha knew in her heart that Jesus could overcome any circumstance.

I Am the Resurrection

Please notice that you will not see Jesus verbally interacting with anyone else in this story on this same level. Martha stood tall. She was not perfect, but her faith cried out, needing to be embraced, and she received what she needed. I can see Jesus looking into her face while saying: "Your brother will rise again" (v. 23). Once again, Jesus did not fully elaborate on his words. In fact, his words were not enough to open Martha's mind up to what was about to happen. Jesus was not attempting to remove all the mental challenges surrounding the situation. Martha did not need to fully understand everything in order to be faithful to him, and Jesus was not under any obligation to fully explain everything to her. He was God. She was not. Can it not be said that the presence of faith automatically acknowledges that a full understanding may remain just out of reach? As a matter of fact, the state of not knowing is the fertile ground in which faith can flourish. It is where faith can reach beyond the darkness and encounter God. In particular, God has chosen faith as the medium whereby we can touch Him.

It appears that Jesus was looking far beyond the fact that Lazarus, his friend, would rise from the dead in the next few moments. One must not lose sight that Lazarus' resurrection would only serve as a demonstration of the resurrection to come.

> "Yes," Martha said, "when everyone else rises, on resurrection day." Jesus told her, "I am the resurrection and the life. Those who believe in me, even though they die like everyone else, will live again. They are given eternal life for believing in me and will never perish. Do you believe this, Martha?" (vs. 24–27)

Martha's faith was rewarded with a beautiful interaction between her and her Lord. Jesus never berated her for her lack of understanding, or for her improper accusation aimed against him. He only strengthened her faith. He never chided her.

Martha was the perfect example of a believer learning to walk by faith. She looked to him through her pain.

We seldom know as much as we would like to know, but through Martha's exchange with Jesus we know that God is not looking for perfection in knowledge and understanding. He is, however, looking for a faith that refuses to be extinguished by the trials and tribulations encountered in this life. Martha's faith was rewarded. The Master smiled upon her faith. He explained to her the powerlessness of death. "Those who believe in me, even though they die like everyone else, will live again. They are given eternal life for believing in me and will never perish" (vs. 25–26). Martha's heart glorified God when her mind said all was lost. She was a woman of unparalleled faith; she stood when others could not, and she won her master's approval. Jesus had the words of life, and he directed them toward Martha.

Jesus finished their conversation with a question: "I am the resurrection and the life . . . Do you believe this, Martha?" (vs. 25–26). Jesus required Martha to look beyond the sting of death; she needed to know that he was the Resurrection of Life. The resurrection power was based on the Son of God who was the embodiment of the resurrection. Jesus was pushing Martha's faith to look beyond her immediate loss because the purpose of raising Lazarus from the dead reached far beyond her immediate family (Sloyan, 1988, p. 144). Jesus challenged her faith in an effort to strengthen her faith. Her faith needed to be anchored in him; he was the manifestation of the resurrection. To believe in Jesus was to embrace the resurrection. Her faith was not only rewarded by Jesus, but it was also being strengthened by him.

Did you notice that Jesus personalized his question to Martha? He did not say: "Do you believe this?" It is important to notice that Jesus said: "'Do you believe this, Martha?'" (v. 26). Jesus was being personal. He wanted her to be personal. Jesus wanted to focus her faith; he wanted to direct her faith on what was important. Jesus wanted her attention to be upon him. He was "the resurrection and the life." To know Jesus, to believe in him, was to have eternal life. What Jesus was about to do for Lazarus he could do for anyone who believed in him.

This exchange between Jesus and Martha was beautiful; it was glorious. Search the entire eleventh chapter of the Gospel of John and you will not see this beautiful exchange between Jesus and anyone else. Martha's faith was still alive and, therefore, she still had ears that were functioning. Her confession of Christ was priceless. She was the one who glorified Jesus, and the Scriptures recorded her success. Adversity had not been successful in stripping her resiliency of faith; it was still alive. She believed in her Lord; Jesus stood taller in her eyes than death. Martha believed.

In verse 28, we read: "Then she left him and returned to Mary. She called Mary aside from the mourners and told her, 'The Teacher is here and wants to see you.'" This entire resurrection story portrays Martha as having the more spiritually mature perspective. It was Martha who Jesus incorporated into his ministry. He wanted to meet with Mary as he had with Martha. So Jesus sent Martha to get Mary. Who is normally sent to get whom? Are the immature sent to get the mature, or are the more spiritually mature sent to get the less mature? Martha stood and talked with Jesus while Mary sat in the house. Martha went when she heard that Jesus was coming without needing to be personally called. Mary needed a personal invitation: "The Teacher is here and wants to see you" (v. 28).

> So Mary immediately went to him. Now Jesus had stayed outside the village, at the place where Martha met him . . . When Mary arrived and saw Jesus, she fell down at his feet and said, "Lord, if you had been here my brother would not have died." When Jesus saw her weeping, and saw the other people wailing with her, he was moved with indignation and was deeply troubled. (vs. 29–33)

What a contrast between Martha and Mary! Where were Mary's words of faith? Where was the faith that peaked out through the pain and loss? Where was the faith that refused to be crushed? Where was the faith that kept her standing? Where was the faith that kept her ears open? Why did our Lord fail to speak? There was no dialogue between Jesus and Mary. She expressed no words of confidence in her Lord. Jesus didn't have any words because Mary didn't have any ears. Who would Jesus have spoken to? Mary was on the ground weeping because death had spoken and there was nothing anyone could do about it. O death, O death, thou hast spoken. Jesus had arrived too late. Death had arrived before Jesus. Mary was glorifying death; she was insulting her Lord. She was dumping indignation upon his head.

After Martha summoned her sister, Mary got up quickly to go meet with Jesus, but Mary went for all the wrong reasons. First, she should have gone earlier. Second, Jesus should not have had to send Martha after her. Third, Mary did not come to talk; she came to give Jesus a piece of her mind. Let's face it. Jesus had disappointed her, he had let her down, and she wanted him to know it. She was hurting and she wanted him to feel her pain. Her reasons for coming were all wrong. If you find that difficult to grasp, meditate or ponder over the event. There is a drastic difference between the sisters' interaction with Jesus. In Mary's case, her arrival was late, she needed to be personally summoned, she threw her accusations at Jesus, and she failed to remain standing with open ears. Jesus' arrival had no positive effect upon her grief, and she did not wait for Jesus to respond. In the light of all of this unbelief, Jesus "was moved with indignation and was deeply troubled" (v. 33). Jesus was personally insulted by this display of unbelief.

The Scriptures do not record Jesus' response with Martha in this manner. Jesus was not moved with indignation or troubled with Martha's actions. Martha went to meet Jesus immediately.

She did come with her accusation; however, she remained standing and waiting for her Lord to speak. And Jesus spoke! He spoke because she still had ears that were open. Martha expressed her confidence in Jesus, and he showed compassion, patience, and understanding. Jesus was there for her. He was not moved with indignation; he was not deeply troubled. Martha's faith was alive! The death of her brother disturbed her, but it did not disturb Jesus. He had come to resurrect his friend. Obviously, the only thing disturbing to Jesus was the open display of Mary's unbelief. He calmly told Martha that Lazarus would rise, and he showed no signs of being overwhelmed by grief. Jesus was the master of the situation. He was in control. Jesus knew that he was the embodiment of the resurrection. Lazarus would rise in a few moments. Martha's faith had earned her a beautiful exchange with the Son of God. Mary did not receive one word from Jesus. Mary was shrouded in unbelief and Jesus "was moved with indignation and was deeply troubled" (v. 33).

Jesus came to crush death; he came to strip death of its finality. He came to glorify the Father by stripping death of its undeserved glory. His indignation was aimed at Mary's naked, raw display of unbelief. Jesus would stop Mary's glorification of death. This was deeply troubling to Jesus. Unbelief is the one and only leading cause of eternal damnation. Jesus was not overwhelmed by the presence of death. He would bring life to the situation. He was not overcome with grief when he was talking to Mary. Joy was just around the corner. Jesus had already declared the outcome. God would be glorified. Grief has no place in this setting. Jesus stated this before he had taken one step. He came to conquer the sting of death.

Specifically, Jesus was there to raise Lazarus from his sleep. He came to awaken his friend. He came to conquer death! Remember, Jesus saw death as weak and as powerless as sleep. Jesus was not being overtaken by sympathy or grief. However, he was being affronted by the atmosphere of unbelief. His indignation was aimed at the unbelief—not at what death had accomplished. His friend would be standing before him in just a few moments. Victory was on the doorstep, and Jesus was that victory. He was the Resurrection Power of God. He was the one who was about to wipe every tear away. He was the one who would end sorrow. He was and still is the one who will end death for all who believe in him.

Jesus knew that Mary's time of grief would be short-lived. Her grief was about to be shattered. Jesus wasn't swallowed up with sympathy for her loss. He was there to restore her loss. To have sympathy is to have a level of agreement with the person and/or to offer support. News flash! Jesus wasn't in any kind of an agreement with Mary's defeated perspective. He was disturbed by her unbelief. The Resurrection of Life was not grieving. Death and the grave were no match for him. The grave would never hold Jesus down, and it wasn't about to hold Lazarus down either. Death was powerless. Jesus held all the power.

Yes! Jesus was agitated during his visit with Mary; he was filled with indignation toward the unbelief. He was being assaulted by unbelief. This complete demonstration of unbelief and the open glorification of death was so disturbing to Jesus that he simply said, "Where have you put him?" (v. 34). There was nothing for him to say. No one was listening. It was time for Jesus to put a stop to this foolishness. Glory belonged to his Father and Jesus was about to make the transfer.

> They told Him, "Lord, come and see." Then Jesus wept. The people who were standing nearby said, "See how much he loved him [Lazarus]." But some said, "This man healed a blind man. Why couldn't he keep Lazarus from dying?" And again Jesus was deeply troubled. (vs. 34–38)

Once again there is a large amount of information contained in this short passage above. So, let us begin with care. Just prior to this verse, Jesus had asked for the whereabouts of Lazarus' grave-site. Apparently, all the interactions between Martha, Mary, and Jesus took place somewhere else. As they began to lead Jesus to the gravesite, Jesus wept. Why? Why did he weep? Well, you had better realize that it had nothing to do with any overwhelming sense of loss. Instead, and most assuredly, it was due to the overwhelming amount of unbelief being displayed. Unbelief was most disturbing to Jesus because unbelief carries a set of eternal consequences. In other words, unbelief is the main thing that can make an eternal God weep, and the stench of unbelief was impregnating the air. The mood of the people was a gaseous mixture of a spiritual foulness that Jesus found repulsive. This aroma was saturating the atmosphere with a foul odor. Jesus' weeping and groaning was an expression of his disapproval. "So powerful was Jesus' emotional reaction to the spectacle that he 'shook' (literally, 'troubled himself') under the force of it" (Bruce, 1983, p. 246).

Next, we need to examine the track record of those who had come out to mourn with Mary and Martha. Please notice that they were not too terribly bright—spiritually speaking. Look at what they had to contribute: "The people who were standing nearby said, 'See how much he [Jesus] loved him [Lazarus]'" (v. 36). They were feeling sorry for Jesus. Poor Jesus! Look how much he loved Lazarus. What a terrible loss for Jesus. Really?! They were speaking in past tense. See how much Jesus had loved Lazarus. They were describing Jesus' love as though it had been cut short. According to them, death had ended or terminated the relationship between Jesus and Lazarus. Really?! Death had dealt Jesus with a death-defying blow? Jesus was someone in need of pity? And there was no hope or remedy? Really?!

They had no accurate concept of what was happening. Jesus was just minutes away from raising Lazarus from the dead. Jesus, the Son of God, was weeping from the lethal presence of unbelief. You can nearly feel the pity these Jews were expressing toward Jesus. Oh, how sad! Jesus came too late. But these

Jews were completely off in their estimation of Jesus and the situation. Plus, this was not the first time these same Jews had misinterpreted the situation.

Do you remember their earlier incorrect conclusions when Jesus had sent Martha to go get Mary? Mary rose up quickly to go see Jesus. This same group of mourners incorrectly assumed that Mary "was going to Lazarus' grave to weep" (v. 31). Wrong! Their self-confident assumption was completely in error. They did not possess any gifted insights. Mary got up quickly to go meet Jesus, and he was not at the gravesite. Obviously, Jesus didn't need their pity. Everyone was on the verge of seeing the resurrection power of God in action.

This group of mourners had miscalculated everything; they failed to correctly ascertain who had the power in this situation. Their entire focus was on power. Jesus did not come to prove he had power. He came to do the will of the Father and, in this particular case, that meant allowing death to speak—first. That meant affording Martha and Mary the opportunity to walk by faith regardless of the circumstances. That meant allowing a painful storm to rage against his friends. That meant allowing unbelief to raise its ugly head. That meant permitting unbelief to assault his divinity. Regardless of what anyone thought, Jesus would move at the discretion of God. He was there to demonstrate the resurrection power of God. Jesus would move according to the timing of God, and not one second before. Jesus knew that this sickness with its death-defying grip would be broken. It could not stand before the resurrection power of God.

Without question, unbelief cut deep into the heart of God. There were no words of encouragement for Mary or the mourners. There was no glimmer of faith for Jesus to challenge or to stir up. All the words, all the thoughts, and all the actions of this group of mourners, and the disciples, and Mary were spiritually offensive, slamming into the spiritual sensibilities of Jesus. And Jesus wept! Is it any wonder that Jesus found this spiritual negativity so deeply disturbing that it led to tears? Their unbelief was directed against the omnipotence of God. It was insulting to the holiness of God's character and nature. Who was man to pity God? Who was man to question the power of God? There was but one thing for Jesus to do. He would demonstrate the resurrection power of God; Jesus would call his friend. Lazarus would rise from his sleep; he would be awakened just as Jesus said he would. Death was no match for Jesus.

God Will Be Glorified

The final parts of Jesus' prophecy were unfolding. The time for glorifying death had come to an end. God would be glorified through the work of the Son. Jesus ordered the removal of the stone in front of Lazarus' grave (v. 39). Martha questioned Jesus' command; she felt that the body of her brother would have begun to stink by now (v. 39). Martha's concern did not trouble Jesus. He did not groan or become troubled over her comment. In fact, his reaction was quite the opposite. Once again, Jesus took the time to turn to his faithful friend and answer her. Jesus already knew that Martha's ears were ready to hear, and so he spoke. His words would become sweet music over the years. She would remember his care and his patience. His words would hang in the air, and she would always listen for his voice. They would be a source of encouragement. No one else in this entire story was so blessed. It was Martha and only Martha who held an active ongoing conversation with Jesus.

"So they rolled the stone aside... Then Jesus shouted, 'Lazarus, come out!' And Lazarus came out, bound in graveclothes, his face wrapped in a headcloth. Jesus told them, 'Unwrap him and let him go!'" (vs. 41–44). So the man who had died came forth, bound hand and foot with wrappings, and his face was wrapped around with a cloth.

Now, we have a resurrection and the reason for Lazarus' death. Death did not have the final say. Death did not hold onto its glory. The final parts of Jesus' prophecy quickly followed: "Many of the people who were with Mary believed in Jesus when they saw this happen" (v. 45). Now, the glory which belonged to God all along was finally where it needed to be. And with that, Jesus' prophecy had come true. Lazarus' sickness had resulted in God receiving glory. Jesus demonstrated that he was the resurrection. He was the life. He and those who believed in him could not be contained by death.

Finally, for the first time, everyone could see death for what is was and for what it was not. Death was small for the believer; it was powerless before God. Those who believed Jesus had a new view of the Son of God and of death. Jesus was truly the Resurrection Power of God. He was the essence of life. Faith in him could reach beyond the grave.

Truly, Martha had more spiritual depth than what tradition normally affords her. Her faith allowed her to stand. She possessed a powerful faith relationship with Jesus. Death could not swallow her faith. It could not separate her from her Lord. In faith, she stood above her contemporaries, and Jesus blessed her. Martha demonstrated how to walk by faith; she demonstrated how to please God. Jesus was her Lord, and she was his loyal servant. They shared precious moments together that others missed out on. Martha blessed God with her faith, and God blessed Martha for her faith. This story, like so many other events recorded in the Bible, proves that God operates according to his timing and not according to the timing of his servants.

The disciples got it all wrong. If they had listened to the words of Jesus in the beginning of the chapter, the whole resurrection story would have been drastically different. It would have been a time of celebration and anticipation leading up to Lazarus being called out of the grave. Let us learn; we should be listening with great care. Our thoughts need to be aligned with his Word. Our lives should be marked by obedience to the Word of God. Jesus chose the road of total submission. Can we—dare we—do any less?

The resurrection account cannot be brought to its conclusion until we remember another powerful event. "Mary took a twelve-ounce jar of expensive perfume made from essence of nard, and she anointed Jesus' feet with it and wiped his feet with her hair. And the house was filled with fragrance" (John 12:3). Yes! Mary failed to glorify Jesus during this resurrection event, but that dark time does not define Mary's whole life. Obviously, Mary knew that her Lord was worthy of all glory and honor. She had anointed her Lord with an expensive perfume, and it was most likely the most expensive thing she owned. Then, she took her own glory—her hair (1 Corinthians 11:15), and she wiped her Master's feet. The house was filled with the aroma of her worship. Unbelief did not cause her to drop at her Master's feet; in her kneeling before Jesus, she stood firmly in her faith. During this event, the stench of unbelief was missing and only the fragrance of worship could be detected. It filled the whole house; Mary glorified God in an impressive manner. We are all like Mary and Martha. One day we stand, and one day we fall, but God is always there to see that we rise again.

In the final analysis, the resurrection will take place at God's appointed time. No one will be in a position to influence it. The dead will rise at the command of God. Some will come forth to face the Resurrection of the Dead; while others, whose names are found recorded in the Book of Life, will participate in the Resurrection of the Life. Everything will be done based upon what is written (Revelation 20:12–15). Jesus never worked independently. He was following the Father's lead; he was following the Father's will (Sloyan, 1988, p. 150).

The goal of the eleventh chapter of the Gospel of John was to present Jesus as the essence, the fulfillment, and the reality of the Resurrection of God. It was the Father's will that Jesus be seen and understood as the Resurrection of God. All believers can be confident; their faith in Jesus will not fail to produce results. Jesus accomplished everything he was sent to do. The salvation of God is complete. Jesus left us with a message of life if we have ears to hear.

CHAPTER 4

The Resurrection of the Dead

[The Loss]

EVERYONE WHO HAS EVER lived will face one of the two separate and distinctly different resurrections. John 5:29 tells us: "Those who have done good will rise to eternal life, and those who have continued in evil will rise to judgment." In the following three chapters, we will examine both resurrections: the Resurrection of the Life and the Resurrection of the Dead. You will find that each of these resurrections is the complete opposite of the other. The complete bliss associated with the Resurrection of Life is completely unfathomable; it lies far beyond the imagination of humanity (1 Corinthians 2:9), but, then, so does the horror of the resurrection of the dead.

The Bible provides snapshots of both. The Resurrection of Life is filled with wonder and awe. Christians need to remember that this present life is not all there is, and "this world is not our home; we are looking forward to our city in heaven, which is yet to come" (Hebrews 13:14). The participants in the Resurrection of Life will be captivated by the beauty of eternity, yearning to explore its rich splendor.

Not to be outdone, the Resurrection of the Dead will be just as captivating. It will be equally permeated with aspects that will draw out the very breath of its participants. The hints the Bible provides about this resurrection are equally spellbinding. Unfortunately, its participants will not be captivated by its beauty. The wonder and awe associated with the Resurrection of Life will be replaced by an unspeakable horror and an unquenchable–unrelenting desire of the participants to escape. No one will want to explore its dark lifeless interior. There will be no life-sustaining power emanating from God. Instead, "all of the attributes of God are completely withdrawn" (Wiese, 2017, p. 112). Those sentenced to this place will not be there for five to ten years or twenty to twenty-five years. Nor will it be a life sentence without the possibility of parole; it will be an eternal damnation—a time without end. Even after ten thousand years, there will be much more to come. In fact, it will have just begun. The Bible repeatedly warns against this place of death. Frequently, Jesus, himself, warned people of the coming judgment. One of Jesus' warnings is recorded in Matthew 5:29. Jesus wanted people to take the approaching judgment seriously. After all, it was a matter of life and death.

In light of the seriousness, the consequences, and the unalterable nature of each place, the Resurrection of Life and the Resurrection of the Dead need to be explored. Every living creature needs to know where they are heading long before they reach their final destination. For once the gates of eternity are closed, they are closed forever. There will be no turning back and getting it right. As we explore each resurrection, we need to realize that both resurrections share a few characteristics in common, and many more that make them altogether dissimilar, utterly singular in nature. The inhabitants will experience very different environments. It cannot be overstated that the conditions of each resurrection will be polar opposites. While both resurrections are beyond our imagination to fully grasp, the Scriptures do provide enough descriptive elements to allow one to ascertain the favorable and unfavorable conditions of each resurrection.

The questions I will use to guide our search for an understanding of these two different places are: "What criteria will determine which resurrection will be encountered? Will one be able to change things and, if so, at what point? What are the characteristics of each resurrection? What experiences will dominate in the different resurrections? Why does one resurrection contain life-sustaining and life-enriching elements, and the other resurrection does not?" These questions are designed to help everyone prepare for the inevitable. All of us will die, all of us will be resurrected, and all of us will face an eternity. Yet, not all of us will face the same eternal conditions. All of us need to remember that "each of us will have to give a personal account to God" (Romans 14:12).

The Great and Terrible Loss

Once again, it must be noted that the Resurrection of the Dead will be a most wretched place. Nevertheless, all of its participants will have had to work hard against the will of God in order to arrive in this terrible place. Their arrival will clearly be the product of choice. This choice will have been made over and over again throughout the individual's lifetime. One's arrival here will not have been the product of one thoughtless decision, but the by-product of a continued persistent passive or aggressive rejection of God's offer of salvation. In light of this, residents in this place will consist of all those who wanted little to do with God, nothing to do with God, or those who were hostile toward even the idea of God. This resurrection will provide a place where one can be totally free from God and from any divine aspect that emanates from him. There will be no more divine standards, no more moral demands, and no more requirements for right living. Here, in this place, there will no longer be any divine intrusions of any kind because life-sustaining instructions will not be applicable. The dead will have forced their way completely out of God's presence. At last, they will be totally free from God. His persistent, intruding presence will be felt no more. There will be a complete void of any attribute of God. His presence will not mar this God-free environment. The occupants of this place will have finally reached their life's ambition: a place where there is no God.

Consequently, the occupants will not receive any additional divine interventions aimed at altering their course of direction because they will have already arrived at their final destination. No reprieve will appear over the distant horizon to offend them. Their self-determined course will have finally placed themselves far beyond the reach of redemption. Their life-long goal of a reality without God will have been obtained. God will honor their decision, making it final and permanent. It will be a reality without God, but what will that reality look like? What characteristics will such a place possess? Horrifying! Appalling! Lifeless! It will be a place never conceived of by the imagination of humanity. No one will have ever experienced such a ghastly place. When you stop to realize, to ponder the fact that we were created in a world enveloped by life-enhancing elements, no one is really prepared to fathom just how dreadful a world of death would actually be. Death and torment and regret will embrace every pitiful occupant.

> In the beginning God created the heavens and the earth . . . The land was filled with seed-bearing plants and trees, and their seeds produced plants and trees of like kind . . . God created great sea creatures and every sort of fish and every kind of bird . . . God made all sorts of wild animals,

livestock, and small animals, each able to reproduce more of its own kind . . . God created people in his own image: God patterned them after himself . . . God looked over all he had made, and he saw that it was excellent in every way." (Genesis 1:1–31)

Can we truly imagine a place of death from a perspective of life? Not completely, and not without relying on the Word of God which is the very thing the dead want to avoid. In fact, they are rejecting the one thing that could help them gain a glimpse of their final destination. However, the Resurrection of the Dead will not be anything anyone would really want. It will exceed the wildest possible expectations of the dammed, but if people truly want to be liberated from God, it will be the perfect place. There will be freedom from God's divine influence, and freedom from all accountability. If someone wants God completely gone, removed, terminated from their world, it is the perfect destination. This hellish place will not be illuminated by God's divine countenance. It will be forever known as a place of absolute utter darkness (Matthew 25:30).

Even in this current sin-distorted world God's presence is everywhere. His provisions are so prevalent that they are taken for granted. It is God who sustains life (Hebrews 1:3). We benefit by his presence in ways that we cannot imagine, but all of that will change for those who failed to turn toward God's eternal provision—Jesus Christ. Hell will be a place totally unlike our current world. Not one aspect, not one characteristic, not one attribute of God will permeate hell. The author Pink states: "Not only does his Word abound in illustrations of his fidelity in fulfilling his promises, but it also records numerous examples of his faithfulness in making good his threatenings" (1975, p. 70).

The fullness of God can be seen throughout creation. God surely claims, "all the animals of the forest are mine, and I own the cattle on a thousand hills. Every bird of the mountains and all the animals of the field belong to me. If I were hungry, I would not mention it to you, for all the world is mine and everything in it" (Psalm 50:10–12). No one has ever known the total and complete absence of God because the abundance of God currently fills the world from one end to the other. He has not disowned his creation. God fills life with his fullness. How desolate will the second death be? It will beyond our imagination. What experience on Earth can equal the total absence of God? Nothing! If God can make everything utterly full, surely, he has the power to make everything utterly empty. Hell will be that place.

In the following pages, I will attempt to produce a basic description of this spiritually desolate place. This partial glimpse of utter emptiness will come through a simple process of removing at least some of the goodness that currently emanates from God. The justification for this process comes from Jesus' own words: "Let those who are spiritually dead care for their own dead" (Matthew 8:22). Jesus was rejecting any ownership of those who did not believe in him. At another time, he stressed the importance of believing in him: "I am the way, the truth, and the life. No one can come to the Father except through me" (John 14:6). Jesus also quoted from an Old Testament passage when he said: "'Long after Abraham, Isaac, and Jacob had died, God said, 'I am the God of Abraham, the God of Isaac, and the God of Jacob.' So, he is the God of the living, not the dead'" (Matthew 22:32). It needs to be remembered that Abraham, Isaac, and Jacob died trusting in the provision of God that was to come just as the believers die trusting in the provision that came—Jesus Christ. Therefore, Jesus could freely state that the dead have no claim to eternal life. God is not the God of the dead; the dead have no God.

Simply stated, those who die without Christ have no God, and they will be stripped of every good thing they took for granted in this life. Some might want to ask why. The reason for this is simple. Every good thing in life came from God. Consider the following:

1. "Whatever is good and perfect comes to us from God above" (James 1:17).

2. "In the beginning God created the heavens and the earth . . . And God saw that it was good" (Genesis 1:1–4).

3. Then God created the light, the sky, the seas, and the land. "And God saw that it was good" (Genesis 1:3–10).

4. Then God created "every sort of grass and seed-bearing plant" and the world teamed with plant life. "And God saw that it was good" (Genesis 1:11–12).

5. Next, God created the sun, the moon, and the stars. "And God saw that it was good" (Genesis 1:14–18).

6. Then God created all of the sea creatures, the various birds to fill the air, and creatures to dwell upon the face of the earth. "And God saw that it was good" (Genesis 1:20–25).

7. Finally, God created the man and the woman in his own image, and God "saw that it was excellent in every way" (Genesis1:26–31).

Author Pink asks, "Would God be "good" if he punished not those who ill-use his blessing, abuse his benevolence, and trample his mercies beneath their feet?" (1975, p. 76).

Obviously, we live in a world teeming with life. There is life in the sea, life in the air, and life covering the surface of the Earth. Everywhere we look there is life. We are embraced with life at every turn. The heavens are full of the creativity of God.

> The heavens tell of the glory of God. The skies display his marvelous craftsmanship. Day after day they continue to speak; night after night they make him known. They

speak without a sound or a word; their voice is silent in the skies; yet their message has gone out to all the earth, and their words to all the world. (Psalm 19:1–4)

Humankind is surrounded by life. God even provided the light humanity uses to see all the wonders of life. People can see the beauty of the mountains, the majestic quality of the trees, the life-giving lakes and the streams with their trickling sound drifting through the forest, and the fresh clean smell in the air after a spring rain. Many enjoy the sound of the waves lapping at the shoreline or the chill in the night air under the stars, or the thousands of colors that cover the mountains in the fall. And, then, there are the migratory patterns of birds and animals that stand as reminders of God's willingness to sustain life (Hebrews 1:3). How do the birds instinctively know to fly south for the winter or north in the summer? Is it a basic desire or need that God touches each year to get them started? Or, does God trigger it by the seasonal changes? Instinctive patterns are not random. These patterns are not independent of God. Bears don't know when to hibernate and when it's time to wake up. Humankind, in his desire to remove God, calls these activities instincts, but, in reality, it is God's ever-gentle hand guiding these creatures through life. Creation is still impregnated with God's majestic presence. His nature and character are visible everywhere. Anyone whose eyes have not been glazed over by the teaching of man can see the glory of God in nature (Romans 1:18–20). Humanity does not have the power to blot out the glory of God, but, at our peril, we can stubbornly deny God's handiwork.

God's creation still bears his eternal image. His eternal existence is glorified by the longevity of the earth, the stars, the moon, and the sun to mention a few. What has humanity ever made that can compare? Nothing! Take a brief look, and be honest! We were created within time. We are subject to time. Everyone is born, and everyone will die. And everything we make bears our temporal image. Everything humanity makes is short-lived; everything is imbued with our image. Cars break down within months after leaving the showroom. Clothing wears out. Furniture and appliances must be repaired and totally replaced over time. Homes need to be maintained and repaired constantly. Roads require constant upkeep. People are temporal, and everything we make is likewise temporal. An honest comparison between what humankind has made and what God has created leaves us looking small, weak, and inadequate. And we feel qualified to challenge or judge God? How absurd! In addition, humanity's continued refusal to acknowledge the truth of creation will only lead thousands more straight into an existence without creativity and beauty. The road to hell is wide and many are traveling down this superhighway, leaving God's glory behind (Matthew 7:13–14). Who in their right God-given mind would want to throw God and his creativity out?

Creation is full of diversity and wonder. We live in a land that beckons for us to explore. Its richness is unending. When we think we have found it all, we find that there is still more to discover. When we think we know it all, we are reminded that we don't. Humanity's knowledge of science is always changing, ever-increasing. Honest accurate science will be an endless search for truth that will always lead back to God. God is truth (John 14:6). Science is just the searching out of what God has created—that which was called into existence by God (Genesis1:1). Diversity comes from God; wonder comes from God. To reject God is to reject diversity and wonder.

Without God there will be nothing to explore; there will be nothing to beckon humankind forward. On the other hand, with God present, there is always the promise of something more—an endless freedom to search out what God has provided. Do we really want to throw that divine invitation away? God is rich, and he has invited us to join with him.

God is truth. Whereas, evolution is a product of humanity; it is designed to produce a world without God. In time, it will produce a harvest all its own, but it will be a harvest of death—the death of diversity and wonder. Beauty will become a thing of the past, and the awesomeness of life will fade away. The finite will no longer be free to explore the infinite. God's invitation to know him will end. God did not create life merely to restrict us from embracing life. God's creation reveals the complexity, the diversity, and the splendor of God. It is the sin and rebellion of humanity that seeks to limit life, leaving people weeping and gnashing their teeth (Matthew 8:12). "The very nature of God makes Hell as real a necessity, as imperatively and eternally requisite, as Heaven is" (Pink, 1975, p. 106).

The Richness of God's Presence

God created life to be one rich fluid moment followed by another and then another. For example, at night we can see the twinkling of the stars, the splendor of the planets, and the irregularities on the surface of the moon. Yet, even these beautiful things are enhanced when they are shared with another person. We were brought into a world of fellowship where beautiful moments could be shared, enhancing the richness of the experience. How many lovers have snuck out to spend an evening under the night's stars? Or, during the day one can walk with a child and enjoy listening to the sounds of a small creek, while watching the movement of the water over the rocks below. These are the things that enhance the experience of life. Our world is not dull; it is full of life. Humanity was created to thrive in a multitude of relationships. Fellowship is one of the many expressions of God. God wanted humanity to know community, intimacy, faith, hope, and love. And the dead are racing headlong toward bringing all the goodness of God to an end. Why? If the offer of eternal life is neglected, all that is of God will be lost as well. The goodness we see in this world is an expression of

God. To reject God is to reject life. So, I will ask my question again: "Why have so many placed the goodness of God on the endangered species' list?" God is a God of goodness. He is the author and the designer of life and fellowship.

Therefore, God created not just the man, but the woman also. They were both created in the image of God (Genesis 1:26). It is for this reason that we know, understand, and anticipate fellowship, intimacy, and love. It is the fullness of God that we enjoy. This is why we hunger for these things in life. The privilege and the wonder of looking into another person's eyes is a gift from above. We also want to be seen; we want someone to look into our eyes, but it does not stop there either. We want to hold someone's hand, and we want our hand held. We want to laugh in the company of others, and when we need to cry, we want to know that our loved ones are nearby. When we are away on a trip, we confidently envision the moments of joy when we will be reunited with our families. All these things emanate from God. These relational elements flow out from the Trinity. God wants to share his abundance with humanity. Our current relationships are only a shadow of the richness shared between God the Father, God the Son, and God the Holy Spirit. God wants us to learn relationships and to join with him and him with us. God wants us to be one with him (John 17:20–25). Spiritual intimacy is a now thing! "God cares more about our response to His Spirit's leading today, in this moment, than about what we intend to do next year" (Chan, 2009, p. 120).

God wants to share his perfect harmony, his perfect unity, and his diversity with us. These are the things shared between God the Father, God the Son, and God the Holy Spirit. Our days are full of the richness of God, but what would be left if the unmeasurable richness of God was completely removed? The land of the dead will not be enhanced with life-giving elements. The dead will have no life and, therefore, life-enhancing elements and life-enhancing moments will have no place in the land of the dead. There will be no fellowship of any kind; relationships will cease to exist (Alcorn, 2004, p. 28).

We draw strength from the many simple pleasures of life. This is especially true if the moments are shared with a loved one. All of these life-giving moments come from God. It was his plan to create a world full of life. I fully understand that all of these things have been marred by sin, but they are still here to a great degree. Because our world is so rich, only a fool will come to the conclusion and say that there is no God (Psalm 14:1).

In contrast, how will a world of death embrace its occupants? What characteristics will such a place possess? Can we safely assume that all of the "good" things we have taken for granted will continue? No! We dare not. The Scriptures promise us that many "will be cast into darkness, where there will be weeping and gnashing of teeth" (Matthew 8:12). The preceding statement was made to the chosen people of God and, if this can happen to the Israelites, it can and will happen to anyone who dies without a Savior. What happens after this life is over should not be trivialized, minimized, or scoffed at. We do not have the power to alter God's decrees. Our arms cannot reach into the heavens and change the ending of his story. The story belongs to God, and it has already been written. We are but many characters within his story. We enter onto the stage of life by the will of God, and we exit the same way. The writer of Ecclesiastes writes: "There is a time for everything, a season for every activity under heaven. A time to be born and a time to die" (Ecclesiastes 3:1–2). However, during life God does offer his hand in friendship to those humble enough to accept it. God graciously leaves each person with a simple decision: "Do I place my hand into God's hand or do I slap his hand away?"

The First Steps of a Relationship

When I became a Christian many years ago, I did not accept Christ because I had all my questions and concerns answered.

The Resurrection of the Dead - The Loss

Quite to the contrary, I had more questions than answers. I had been told all about our need for salvation. In addition, many other topics had been explained to me concerning the Bible. And, quite frankly, a lot of the claims sounded outlandish. And, as far as I was concerned, many of the claims placed God into one of two categories: either God was a stupid liar, or he was God. At first, as a new Christian, I found myself wishing that God had played his hand a little safer. I knew that the outlandish claims placed a lot of pressure onto God—not me. I was not the one in danger of being caught in a lie, and any lie on God's part would have ended our relationship. I knew that I would not tolerate the presence of a habitual liar. Over the years, I never feared looking at things that appeared to disprove God. Other Christians would ask me: "Why are you looking into this matter?" And I would usually answer with: "If man can dethrone God, then God is not much of a God. Plus, God should not need the help of any man, including myself, in order to maintain his throne." This reality left me free to explore. I did not have to hide my eyes. I could look intently into any issue that arose.

In addition, as a new Christian, I could not see the wisdom in outright rejecting Christ from a position of ignorance. To outright reject that which I did not know seemed unintelligent to me—rather stupid. So, in my usual candid manner, I informed God that he had left himself with little to no wiggle room. There was simply no middle ground for God, and I knew that time would reveal the truth about God. If God turned out to be a liar, I would have no use for him, and I would try to become his worst enemy. If God turned out to be God, then I would be his. I knew from experience that a person will either verify the good things you heard about them, or they will disprove the good report.

Obviously, all relationships begin this same way. All new relationships begin with a step of faith; we decide to step out and trust someone. All new relationships are subject to experience and our ability to reason through situations over time. If a person proves that they are honest, if a person proves that they are reliable, if a person turns out to be what they claimed to be, then the relationship has the opportunity to flourish. If not, one is totally free to terminate the relationship. This process is the same with God. The real danger is that some reject God before they ever begin a relationship with him, fearing that God may be too controlling or too demanding or too something. Whatever the case, rejecting God is rejecting God.

God has taken the first step in reaching out to humanity through the life and death of Jesus Christ. The Son of God laid down his life in an offer of friendship. Now, humankind is the one under an obligation to respond to God's offer of eternal life. People can either accept the offer or reject the offer. If an individual accepts God's offer of friendship and God turns out to be less than God, then that individual is free to terminate the relationship. No one is required to maintain a relationship with a liar, and no one is required to maintain a relationship based upon abuse. But, if a person outright rejects God's offer of eternal life, then that person will face the consequences resulting from their actions. Every decision must be made with great care. Everyone must remember that there is no life outside of God. Separation from God is the equivalent to a death sentence. Therefore, one must take into account that the process of relationship building or the consequences of rejecting a relationship are the same whether that action is with another person or with God. However, with God the stakes are much higher. In light of these facts, there is no legitimate reason for anyone to reject Jesus Christ without some reasonable effort to know him. God's offer of friendship is an eternal offer of friendship—to reject his offer will be eternal as well. Deep contemplation should precede action.

Death's Embrace

So, back to our questions: "How would a world of death embrace its occupants? What characteristics will such a place possess?" According to Revelation, " anyone whose name was not found recorded in the Book of Life was thrown into the lake of fire" (20:15). That statement is alarming. If one's passage into eternity is not punched with a clear destination of eternal life, then the second death will become a reality. In fact, the shadow of death hangs over everyone who has not accepted God's provision for life.

For those found written in the Book of Life, God has already removed the death penalty. He has removed sorrow, crying, and pain from their eternity (Revelation 21:4), but these elements will go unchecked in the land of dead. For in a land of death, there will be no divine presence to hold back the onslaught of loss. Death will abound. Sorrow will abound. Crying will know no end. Pain will fill every moment. The dead will know no relief from this unrelenting torment. The eternal loss of all aspects of life will cause deprivation to permeate every crevice. The inhabitants of this dreadful place will lose everything, including that which they valued, that which they cherished, and that which they took for granted. Every good thing will be gone (Alcorn, 2004, p. 28). And in its place will be an eternal darkness. The darkness will be like a thick blanket of gel, leaving the soul gasping in an endless void. Painful unending screaming will shred the vocal cords, and "there will be weeping and gnashing of teeth" (Matthew 8:12). The wicked will not get the last laugh. Their laugh may have been long and it may have been hard, but it will prove to have been empty. True wholesome laughter is the by-product of enjoying life, but the laughter of the wicked is the by-product of taking life from someone else. It is the by-product of evil intentions and evil deeds. This kind of laughter does not add to life; it is empty, cold, and lifeless. It is a laughter that will turn to "weeping and gnashing of teeth" (Matthew 8:12).

I started to say that the damned will have no relief, day or night, but that would have been an improper statement. There will be no light and, therefore, no daylight in the land of the dead.

God is light, and he will not be there to roll back the darkness. Plus, it needs to be remembered that the concept of day and night are associated with the passage of time, and the dead have no need for understanding the passage of time. The dead will only know darkness—uninterrupted perpetual darkness. Why? Again, because God is light; he is the "one who is the true light" (John 1:9). The dead have rejected light because "they loved the darkness more than the light" (John 3:19). The dead have no God, and with the total absence of God there will be no light. Without light there will only be the darkness. The damned will be eternally held in the embrace by an utter captivating darkness. There will be no beauty to behold, no trees blowing in the wind, and no clouds passing overhead. There will be no signs of life anywhere. There will be no looking out the window, no deer standing in the front yard, no children playing in the snow, and no sunrise or sunsets—just the constant darkness. With no relief in sight from the darkness, " there will be weeping and gnashing of teeth" (Matthew 8:12).

Again, Revelation states; "Blessed are those who are invited to the wedding feast of the Lamb" (19:9). The dead will not be invited to this feast because their names were not found written in the Book of Life. In fact, the dead are never associated with the word *blessed*. The feast mentioned in Revelation acknowledges a standing relationship with God. It is a time of fellowship, rejoicing, a gathering together, a time of celebration, a reunion, and a time to share old stories and triumphs. All of these things are components that enrich life, and the dead have no life to be enriched. The dead have no relationship with God and are, therefore, not entitled to a time of fellowship. There will be no celebrations or reunions. Feasting is a jubilant part of life; it is an enriching activity that binds people together. The dead will not pull up a chair and attend God's banquet. There will be no bonding among the dead. Death will be the only companion of the dead. There will be no elements of enrichment for the dead. A feast would be out of the question and out of place. A feast can denote a time of public praise and honor for past accomplishments. This will not happen for the dead because they allowed their sinful past to swallow their present and their future.

Humans were originally created to be in fellowship with the creator (Genesis 3:8–9). In that state, people were free to learn about the immeasurable love of God the Father, God the Son, and God the Holy Spirit. Humanity had been invited into the intimate love relationship of God. Love is unique and beautiful, but it will not force itself upon another. Love brings freedom and life, but it is subject to the openness of its intended recipient. Love can be rejected; God's love can be rejected. Unbelievers demand to live outside of God's love, beyond God's love, and if they insist long enough, God will comply. The unbelievers can find themselves with an eternity based upon their own making and, in this place, there will be no fellowship, there will be no comrades (Alcorn, 2004, p. 28). There will be no rulers or followers. There will be no friends or enemies. Occupants in this terrible place will never see their former husbands or wives. They will never see their children, their moms, or their dads. There will be no social groups of any kind. There will be no police or preachers, and the most tragic of all—there will be no God. The dead have no God. The concept of being buried alive will have a new and terrifying meaning. The memories of the past will fade—all will be lost.

Time Is Coming to an End

Do you remember the account of the rich man waiting for the judgment of God in Luke 16:19–26?

> Jesus said, "There was a certain rich man who was splendidly clothed and who lived each day in luxury. At his door lay a diseased beggar named Lazarus. As Lazarus lay there longing for scraps from the rich man's table, the

dogs would come and lick his open scores. Finally, the beggar died and was carried by the angels to be with Abraham. The rich man also died and was buried, and his soul went to the place of the dead. There, in torment, he saw Lazarus in the far distance with Abraham. The rich man shouted, 'Father Abraham, have some pity! Send Lazarus over here to dip the tip of his finger in water and cool my tongue, because I am in anguish in these flames.' But Abraham said to him, 'Son, remember that during your lifetime you had everything you wanted, and Lazarus had nothing. So now he is here being comforted, and you are in anguish. And besides, there is a great chasm separating us. Anyone who wanted to cross over to you from here is stopped at its edge, and no one there can cross over to us.'" (Luke 16:19–26)

There are several things to be noted in the passage above. First, the rich man in Jesus' story was not identified by his given name, and that was because the dead have no names. Names are used to identify different individuals in relationships, and the dead have no relationships. Second, the former rich man begged for a drop of water to be placed upon his scorched tongue, but, in reality, the man was asking for far more than a single drop of water. He was deeply thirsty, desiring to participate in life—even if it was for just a few moments. You see, in order for someone to bring him water, several life-giving components would have had to come into play, and he was beyond life-giving action. Therefore, no action could be entered into on his behalf because that would have placed him right back into a relationship setting. And the rich man was numbered among the dead.

To bring him water, Lazarus would have been offering him compassion and care. And these are components of life, and the rich man had already passed beyond the opportunity for compassion and care. Similarly, to bring him water would be the equivalent of bringing him relief from suffering, and there is no relief in the land of the dead. This place is a land of no names, no identities, no relationships, and no life-sustaining measures of any kind. It is a place of unspeakable horror.

Equally important is the concept of hope. Hope has at least two important elements embedded within it. There must be the thing hoped for, and a way to gain the thing hoped for, or someone who can grant the thing hoped for. So, the concept of hope is obviously only found in life-giving and life-sustaining situations. To hope for something is to anticipate the thing hoped for. To hope is to dream, to long for with an element or measure of obtaining the thing hoped for. It doesn't take long to realize that hope is rooted in life. Hope enhances life, adding an element of expectation. Hope gives the eyes something to focus upon. Hope is powerful enough to lift up the eyes, but, when hope fails, the eyes grow dim and one's countenance falls.

In short, the dead have no hope. Hope cannot sustain itself; it cannot survive in a place of death. The Book of Proverbs tells us: "When the wicked die, their hopes all perish, for they rely on their own feeble strength" (11:7). Simply put, the dead do not have the power to sustain hope. Hope is the by-product of relationships, and the dead have no relationships. What happens to hope when it goes unanswered? What happens to unanswered hope after one year, after ten years, after one hundred years, or after ten thousand years? Unanswered hope means that there is no one out there who will assist you. "Everything we have is because of the generosity of God" (Jeremiah, 2016, p. 98). But what happens when God's generosity is lost? Desperation invades! The hopeless are smothered in torment with no relief, no reprieve, and no expectation of a future. Tomorrow is lost. The sun will not rise again. There is only the darkness—that lifeless blackness of the eternally damned.

Again, we must mention the rich man from above. He was in torment, waiting to be judged. He had not yet been thrown out into outer darkness. He could see from afar that others were participating in life. There was a "great chasm" between him and the living, and no one could cross over to him (Luke 16:26). It was impossible for anyone to bring him anything, and, if someone had, it would have been misleading. It would have been a false hope; a hope that promised more and more would not be delivered. The former rich man would not receive one molecule of hope. Search the Bible through, hope is associated with God and with those who believed in him. Those without God "will be condemned at the time of the judgment" (Psalm 1:5). The end of the damned is hopeless destruction. The "Lord watches over the path of the godly, but the path of the wicked leads to destruction" (Psalm 1:6). The "Lord is righteous, and he loves justice. Those who do what is right will see his face" (Psalm 11:7).

According to the verse above, those who do right will see the face of God. So, what is right? What does God consider right? A crowd once approached Jesus and asked a question very similar. "'What does God want us to do?' Jesus told them, 'This is what God wants you to do: Believe in the one he [God the Father] has sent'" (John 6:28–29). This was a straightforward question followed with a direct answer by Jesus. There was nothing ambiguous with the question, and there was nothing obscure with Jesus' response. We read in John: "God did not send his Son into the world to condemn it, but to save it. There is no judgment awaiting those who trust him. But those who do not trust him have already been judged for not believing in the only Son of God" (3:17–18). Hope belongs to those who believe in Jesus. Their hope rests in God; he is the source of their hope. He is the sustainer of their hope. God's eternal strength keeps their hope alive. All outside of God's fellowship will express their lack of hope with "weeping and gnashing of teeth" (Matthew 8:12).

Finally, we come to the biggest questions of them all: "Where does the concept of love fit into the picture? Can love be given and received in hell?" No! To be honest, it does not appear to be likely even in the smallest degree. Jesus made the following statement shortly before he was crucified: "Those who obey my commandments are the ones who love me" (John 14:21). The dead fail to obey the commandments of Jesus. They spurned the love of God. God sent his Son into the world because of his great love for the world (John 3:16), but so many were not interested in the love of God. Their refusal to obey the commandments of God was an equivalent to denying God, and Jesus clearly stated that anyone who denied God would be denied by him at the judgment (Matthew 10:33). This will be a terrible loss—a loss far greater than any other. Nearly everyone would cry, if they lost their mother's love, yet the source of her love is God. How much more will people weep and grind their teeth over the loss of God's love? Yet, the only way to lose his love is to reject his love.

In other words, the time and the opportunity to be loved by God and to love God is over for the dead. Instead of being welcomed into the loving arms of God, the damned will be cast out (Matthew 13:50). In the life of the believer, the Holy Spirit is the source of their "love, joy, peace, patience, kindness, goodness, faithfulness, gentleness, and self-control" (Galatians 5:22). With the dead having no God from which to draw from, what will be their source for all these things? God has been the source of man's community, fellowship, and intimacy. These are all extensions offered from the relationship within the Trinity. Without God's presence and divine nature, all the "good" things in life disappear. The dead won't have anyone to love them nor will they have anyone to love. Love without action is unexpressed love; it will die. Love enhances life, and there will be no life in hell. I'm afraid that there will "be weeping and gnashing of teeth" (Matthew 8:12).

In conclusion, any person leaving this world without Christ as their Lord and Savior are headed for a place of death. Throughout the Scriptures, no matter where one may look, you will never find God associating the word *good* with terms like: *second death* or *lake of fire* or *outer darkness* or *cast out* or *bottomless pit*.

It is never good to fall into the hands of an angry God. The Psalms clearly records God's perspective: "God is a judge who is perfectly fair. He is angry with the wicked every day" (Psalm 7:11). The Scriptures further state that God will not share our affection with anything else (Exodus 20:5). Again, the Scriptures are explicit: "Anyone who isn't helping me [Jesus] opposes me, and anyone who isn't working with me is actually working against me" (Matthew 12:30). The words of God are plain and straightforward; there will be no misunderstandings. As the writer of Hebrews asks: "What makes us think that we can escape if we are indifferent to this great salvation that was announced by the Lord Jesus himself?" (2:3).

Jesus, the Son of God, had a reason for coming. He did not lay down his life because he thought it would be fun. Judgment is surely coming to everyone. No one is exempt, "And just as it is destined that each person dies only once and after that comes judgment, so also Christ died only once as a sacrifice to take away the sins of many people" (Hebrews 9:27–28). Jesus, the Son of God, brought eternal life, only he could lay down his life and offer eternal life to everyone who believed in him (John 1:1–14). It is only the blood of Jesus that is capable of separating individuals from their sin, making that person acceptable in the eyes of God (Romans 3:23–26).

Now, the ball is in your court. How will you respond? Will you accept the hand of God in friendship, or will you slap his hand away? God is life and, if you reject God, you reject life. Your eternity lies in the balance, whether you like it or not. Please choose wisely. Through the work of Christ, heaven is open to you and hell is closed to you; but, if you close the door to heaven, hell will beckon to you with its mouth wide open. Many have passed through its gates never to return. The offer of divine friendship is real. The Bible appears to have made many statements that appear to be outlandish from a human perspective, but that only gives you the opportunity to search out God and know if he is a liar or not. This places you in a position where you can reasonably determine if the offer is valid, but you really cannot make a reasonable decision without some degree of personal investment. Any new relationship contains an element of the unknown. Any new relationship requires a step of faith that must be coupled with reason, experience, and time. It is no different with God; it is the same process.

The rich man mentioned above chose to go his own way. He did not make time for God. God was not important enough. Nevertheless, the rich man did not want to see his brothers follow in his footsteps, and end up in a place of torment like him. He knew that nothing could be done to help him. His fate was already sealed; he would wait in torment for God's final judgment to descend upon him. So, he called out to Abraham, begging for a special warning to be sent to his brothers, but Abraham denied his request, stating that his brothers had the Scriptures available to them (Luke 16:27–31). You may be waiting for God to meet some special set of circumstances or conditions before you are willing to believe in Jesus. Good luck with that. You, like the rich man's brothers, have the Scriptures available to you. I personally hope you choose wisely! Eternity is drawing nearer every day and with it comes the final judgment. You really must not delay.

CHAPTER 5

The Resurrection of the Dead

[The Judgment]

THE RESURRECTION OF THE Dead is not a bad thing! It is just, and, therefore, it is good and right. It will be a time of reckoning. Satan and his hoard of demons will come face-to-face with justice. The Scriptures are clear in that God hates evil.

> O God, you take no pleasure in wickedness: you cannot tolerate the slightest sin. Therefore, the proud will not be allowed to stand in your presence, for you hate all who do evil. You will destroy those who tell lies. The Lord detests murderers and deceivers. (Psalm 5:4–6)

Jesus characterized Satan by openly stating that Satan "was a murderer from the beginning and has always hated the truth. There is no truth in him. When he lies, it is consistent with his character; for he is a liar and the father of lies" (John 8:44). Satan will be ultimately destroyed for being a liar—the father of all lies.

The former archangel will be judged! That which is evil must meet its just end or God is not just. Therefore, Satan's current ability to rule over his demonic hoard is temporary.

As a created creature, Satan had a beginning, and he will have an end. His evil intentions have guaranteed him a front row seat in the final judgment. His time is finite. His right to bring destruction is defined by the parameters of his beginning and his end. Thank God that his satanic rule will be utterly destroyed. His kingdom will fall. In fact, his self-exalted status was doomed before it ever began. Evil cannot remain; it must have an end. If God's justice fails to prevail, then God has failed, and that will mean that God has fallen short of being right. At the Great White Throne Judgment evil will be silenced once and for all, and all who stand clothed in evil will be damned to a place of torment (Matthew 2:29).

It is a shame that Satan, so highly placed and honored, gambled for more. He coveted God's glory. His plan was to exalt himself and to become the equal of God (Isaiah 14:14). In so doing, he became the father of pride and greed, and Satan should serve as a reminder to all who seek after that which rightfully belongs to another. The cost of evil is high. You could end up losing everything—even that which was once originally and rightfully yours. And that loss will prove to be only part of what is to come. Throughout all eternity that uncontrollable aching need to covet what did not belong to him may become a part of the eternal torment he will face. To be haunted, to be driven, by a deep-seated lusting for what will never be may be the most tormenting self-inflected aspect of all. Sin inherently carries a penalty. Satan and all of his demons understood this reality. They once stood in the very presence of God Almighty. The Gospels inform us that the demons know that the justice of God is quickly approaching. They are tormented by this fact; the eternal fires were prepared for them and their vanquished king (Matthew 25:41).

Therefore, it stands to reason that Satan will not be the lord of hell; he will no longer be in charge of his demons. The demons will not be doing any of Satan's bidding. Satan will be in the land of torment; he will be preoccupied and consumed with his own tormented state. Neither he nor his demons will be in a position to administer torment to others. They won't be in charge! Hell was created for them! The fires of hell are their place of judgment. Nowhere in the Scriptures do we find the demons or Satan singing: "We will get to go to hell. We will play in the fire." The demons were not looking forward to going to hell. Upon seeing Jesus, the demons "began screaming at him [Jesus], 'Why are you bothering us, Son of God? You have no right to torture us before God's appointed time!'" (Matthew 8:29). The demons were literally tormented by the concept of God's approaching judgment. Eternal darkness will not be the domain where Satan and his demons rule; it will be their eternal judgment.

Therefore, one can rest assured that the demons were not anticipating the joys of hell; they were not anticipating the pleasure of being able to torment any other occupants of hell. All demonic powers will vanish; they will be powerless! There will be a complete and everlasting void in their power. Satan's temporary rule will terminate. Satan will be a dethroned king in everlasting torment. God will not exalt him and set him up as the warden of hell. His demons will not function as tormenting guards. That would bring them pleasure, and hell is not a place of pleasure. Satan and his hoard will exist in the shadow of God's eternal judgment, and it will be just.

The angels were created to serve in the eternal presence of God. They personally knew God. They beheld his eternal glory; they saw his creative power. They stood in the midst of God's majestic wonder and awe. Nevertheless, Satan and one-third of the angels rebelled against God (Revelation 12:3–4). They rebelled against their God-given boundaries; they "did not stay within the limits of authority God gave them" (Jude 1:6). Their aim was to overthrow their God and Creator. "They wanted to dominate, and that desire continues to be their main motivation today" (DeStefano, 2020, p. 122). Again, we may rest assured in that God will never honor their desire to dominate or torment any part of his creation ever again. Their sick evil desires will end; it will burn with them for all eternity. Their demonic desire to rule will never be gratified. The great battle they lost in heaven was just the beginning.

> Then there was war in heaven. Michael and the angels under his command fought the dragon and his angels. And the dragon lost the battle and was forced out of heaven. This great dragon—the ancient serpent called the Devil, or Satan, the one deceiving the whole world—was thrown down to the earth with all his angels. (Revelation 12:7)

Satan was thrown out of heaven at the end of the battle. And the time is coming when Satan and his hoard will be thrown into the eternal flames prepared for them. There is no grace or forgiveness for them. Their fate is sealed; they have no savior. The Scriptures do not outline any plan on the part of God to provide the fallen angels with a way to escape their final judgment. There is no qualified mediator between God and the fallen angels. They are approaching the judgment of God. Hell is their reality! "Without hell, the war between good and evil wouldn't be a war at all" (DeStefano, 2020, p. 189). Good must have a final triumphant outcome. God will prevail! Satan will be crushed!

Jesus did not take on the likeness of an angel when he came to Earth. However, he did take on the likeness of humanity (Romans 8:3). Jesus "became human and lived here on earth among us. He was full of unfailing love and faithfulness" (John 1:14). Jesus brought new life from heaven for the benefit of humankind. "Humans can reproduce only human life, but the Holy Spirit gives new life from heaven" (John 3:6). This new life from heaven came through the person of Jesus Christ. Jesus was both human and divine, bridging the gap between God and man. As Paul writes: "For there is only one God and one Mediator who can reconcile God and people. He is the man Christ Jesus. He gave his life to purchase freedom for everyone" (1 Timothy 2:5–6). This provision of salvation through Jesus Christ applies toward all of humanity—not the fallen angels.

This is the fear factor behind the response of the demons when they encountered the Son of God. They knew their end. The demons repeatedly revealed their powerless position before God Almighty. The Gospels give us many pictures of this. "That evening many demon-possessed people were brought to Jesus. All the spirits fled when he [Jesus] commanded them to leave" (Matthew 8:16). Jesus "rebuked the evil spirit . . . Then the spirit screamed and threw the boy into another violent convulsion and left" (Mark 9:25–26). "The demons kept begging Jesus not to send them into the Bottomless Pit" (Luke 8:31). On another occasion, Jesus was teaching in Capernaum, and "a man possessed by a demon began shouting at Jesus, 'Go away! Why are you bothering us, Jesus of Nazareth? Have you come to destroy us? I know who you are—the Holy One sent from God'" (Luke 4:33–34).

Even in human form the demons could recognize the divine presence of God, and this tormented them. Jesus' humanity did not obscure his divine identity, and his holy presence reminded them of their coming judgment. They knew there was no provision, and they responded with fear and torment. The earthly ministry of Jesus marked a massive passage of time. The age where demons could freely roam the face of the earth was coming to a close. Time was short. Their final judgment rose up with the rising of the Son of God.

Without a doubt, their fear was well-founded. The judgment of God will be just as terrible and complete as his gracious forgiveness will be glorious and unmeasurable. Hell will be a place of torment, and hell's demonic occupants will know an eternal catastrophe. Did you notice the overwhelming desire of the demons to remain within God's creation? They did not want to be cast out. They were willing to beg for a dwelling place amidst a herd of pigs. Being in and a part of a smelly nasty herd of pigs was much more desirable than their final destination. They did not want to be "cast out" (Matthew 8:30). The demons did not want to be cast out of God's creation and into the "Bottomless Pit" (Luke 8:31). Twisted, evil, and fallen, the demons still wanted to remain within God's creation. They had already lost heaven, and the earth would be their next terrible loss. Therefore, a home within a herd of pigs was still far more preferable than losing every trace of God's presence. To be sure, hell will be a place where the total absence of God will be experienced. And God's divine absence will be forever missing. It will be a place without time, a place of unending torment. There will be no river of life flowing through the land where they are going. Their land will be stark and lifeless.

In contrast, those in the land of the living will be experiencing the emergence of the New Heaven and the New Earth. All that was touched and tainted by sin will have passed away (Revelation 21:1). The holy city of God, "the new Jerusalem," will descend from heaven down to the earth (Revelation 21:2). The city will be illuminated by the glory of God, and his glory will remove the need to close the gates—darkness will not touch the city (Revelation 21:23–25). The gates will remain open twenty-four hours every day. Nothing will close down God's holy city. The people will see and know the One whom Satan and his demons attempted to overthrow. The redeemed will see God's glory—that which the demons wanted for themselves. Throughout all eternity, the redeemed will have that which Satan threw away. The people will see the river of life "flowing from the throne of God and of the Lamb, coursing down the center of main street" (Revelation 22:1–2). Death will be a thing of the past; evil will be "gone forever" (Revelation 21:4). The presence of God will illuminate every aspect of life for the redeemed, but the cast-out ones will be in total darkness—a place entirely unlike God. The demons will long for the days when they could have dwelt among a herd of pigs.

Darkness will grip the land of the dead with a thick blanket of desolate blackness (2 Peter 2:17, Jude 13). It may be similar to the Earth before God started his acts of creation "at which time" light and life were impregnated into every aspect of this world. "The earth was empty, a formless mass cloaked in darkness. And the Spirit of God was hovering over its surface" (Genesis 1:2). At this point in the account of creation, there was not even the hint of any element of life—"the earth was empty, a formless mass cloaked in darkness." The description was perfect. It was a lifeless, formless, mass enveloped in darkness, but the Spirit of God hovered above it with his creative powers. And life came into being. Unfortunately, God will not hover over hell with his creative powers of light and life. Hell will be a place of death (Luke 12:4–5)—not benefitting from any life-enhancing elements. Satan and his demons will never see the light of God ever again. The endless darkness of the damned will be what they inherit from their sin.

The darkness will be a complete and perfect void of light. It will be thick, filling every crevice of the body. It will engulf and encase the occupants of hell, making each one an isolated uninhabited point in the darkness—a lifeless island in a black sea of nothing. The aloneness of hell will be deafening; it will be absolute silence. There will be nothing on the distant horizon to foster hope. Eyes will be unable to see what is not there. The stench of hell will assault their senses; the sickening pungent smell will be their own sinful self burning in the eternal fires. When the damned breathe, it will be an inhalation of scorching heat and fire. The tongue will be a thing of constant agony (Luke 16:24). The ears of the dead will be filled with their own wrenching screams. In addition, the dead will have their sense of touch enveloped in pure unending torment. Hell will be the fulfillment of God's enduring judgment—designed for Satan and his demonic hoard. It is difficult to understand why anyone would ever choose to go to the wretched place. This was to be Satan's eternal place of torment—not humanity's. "God never intended for man to go there" (Wiese, 2017, p. 131). Any man or woman that ends up in hell is an intruder into a place designed for Satan.

In contrast, those in the land of the living will be experiencing the fullness of God. God will bless "those who realize their need for him, for the Kingdom of Heaven is given to them" (Matthew 5:3). God will bless "those who mourn, for they will be comforted" (Matthew 5:4). God will bless "those who are gentle and lowly, for the whole earth will belong to them" (Matthew 5:5). God will bless "those who are hungry and thirsty for justice, for they will receive it in full" (Matthew 5:6). God will bless "those who are merciful, for they will be shown mercy" (Matthew 5:7). God will bless "those whose hearts are pure, for they will see God" (Matthew 5:8). God will bless "those who work for peace, for they will be called the children of God" (Matthew 5:9). And, God will bless "those who are persecuted because they live for God, for the Kingdom of Heaven is theirs" (Matthew 5:10).

Those in the land of the living will see their Savior. He will be "wearing a long robe with a gold sash across his chest" (Revelation 1:13). His head and hair will be "white like wool, as white as snow" (Revelation 1:14). His eyes will be radiant like the flames of a fire (Revelation 1:14). His feet will be "bright as bronze refined in a furnace" (Revelation 1:15), and his voice will be like no other; it will thunder "like mighty ocean waves" (Revelation 1:15). And his face will be "as bright as the sun in all its brilliance" (Revelation 1:16). Glory and honor will be his. Darkness will have no place in him. The presence of God will eternally hover over his children, and there will be no more sorrow or crying or pain (Revelation 21:4), There will be no more despair or hopes shattered, nor dreams lost. Aloneness and isolation will have been vanquished to the realm below. All will be excellent!

However, this will not be true for Satan and his demons. They will be the cast-out ones. They will never touch God's creation again, and they will never be touched by God's goodness again. Satan and his demons will be touched by the wrath of God. The fires of hell will have two weaknesses. The fires of hell will neither have the power to produce light nor to end one's existence. Nevertheless, the flames will have the power to permanently burn away any thought of life. They will be able to consume every hope and instantly dry every tear. The tongues of the damned will be parched, and their throats will be cracked and dry. The king of darkness will have his darkness, but there will be no throne. Death in this terrible place will be eternal—never-ending. It is foolishness to think that Satan will be in charge of anything.

Time Is God's Gift

The ill-fated demons knew and demonstrated that they understood that time was not their friend; their time of destruction was drawing nearer and nearer. Clearly, the passage of time only added to their torment. This observation should prompt us to ponder. If time does not serve any purpose for the fallen angels, what does the passage of time accomplish? What is the purpose of time? If the fate of the demons was already fixed, if their fate in the eternal flames was already sealed, who then benefits from the existence of time? That is a question that needs to be answered, but the answer is located in a book many want to avoid. Nevertheless, if answering that question is the goal, then one must look into the one book designed to provide glimpses into the eternal world to come. God's Holy Word holds the key to that question.

God established time in the beginning of creation (Genesis 1:1–5), and "God looked over all he had made, and he saw that it was excellent in every way" (Genesis 1:31). Time is a part of creation, and it is part of that which God called "good." Not only did God create time, but he also placed markers within creation so that the passage of time could be understood.

> And God said, "Let bright lights appear in the sky to separate the day from the night. They will be signs to mark off the seasons, the days, and the years. Let their light shine down upon the earth." And so it was. For God made two great lights, the sun and the moon, to shine down upon the earth. The greater one, the sun, presides during the day; the lesser one, the moon, presides through the night. He also made the stars. God set these lights in the heavens to light the earth, to govern the day and the night, and to separate the light from the darkness. And God saw that it was good. (Genesis 1:14–18)

In other words, God wanted the passage of time to be understood; he set lights in the sky as signs. These signs were to "mark off the seasons, the days, and the years" (Genesis 1:14). God intended for someone to look up and understand the passage of time. Satan and his demons had no need to look up and see the bright lights. They were in heaven at one time; then they were cast down to the Earth. This present world was not created for them, but it was created for humankind. It was to be man's domain (Genesis 1:26–28). Humanity was meant to rule the Earth, but we fell to the same temptation that brought about Satan's demise.

In fact, Satan took the evil from within his own heart and used it on us. And it worked! Satan deceived Adam and Eve, making them think that they could "become just like God, knowing everything, both good and evil" (Genesis 3:5). In one foolish moment, they chose to follow Satan's voice instead of God's,

The Resurrection of the Dead - The Judgment

and with that disastrous decision they entered into rebellion and sin. They followed Satan's lead and, thereby, caused a separation between themselves and God. Unfortunately, their decision would impact all of humanity. "When Adam sinned, sin entered the entire human race. Adam's sin brought death, so death spread to everyone, for everyone sinned" (Romans 5:12). All inherited his sin nature, and all inherited his spiritually separated status from the eternal God.

Therefore, God sent his Son to die that we might live through him (John 3:17), and God's plan of salvation includes every man, woman, and child. We read in the Gospel of John: "For God so loved the world that he gave his only Son, so that everyone who believes in him will not perish but have eternal life" (3:16). God "does not want anyone to perish" (2 Peter 3:9). God's plan was inclusive—Christ died for all. Remember that Jesus, the Son of God, came to earth in the likeness of a man. He came to redeem humanity. The righteous One, Jesus Christ, was willing to die that the *unrighteous*, that means people, might live. We were separated from life; we were separated from God. A death sentence hung over our heads, but that separation ended with the death of Jesus Christ. Jesus is God's provision. Christ removed the spiritual separation, and through believing in him, everyone can have life. People do not have to remain under the penalty of death. Everyone is free to choose life. No one needs to share in Satan's fate. Everyone can be set free by turning to God and accepting his provision for life. God never intended for humanity to enter into that which was prepared for Satan and his demons (Wiese, 2017, p. 131).

All things considered, time becomes one of the many gifts that God has given to us, but it comes with an expiration date. Or, better yet, each of us comes with an expiration date. Everyone has been allotted a specific amount of time in which to turn to God for eternal life. And in this one area God has not treated everyone equally. The time allotted to each person is set long before they were ever born (Jeremiah 1:4–5). The writer of Ecclesiastes tells us: "There is a time for everything, a season for every activity under heaven. A time to be born and a time to die" (3:1–2). Therefore, everyone's day of accountability is approaching at a different rate of speed. Some are only given a few years or moments to make their decision while others have an entire lifetime. No one knows how much time they have, and no one has any say in the matter. We are born at an appointed time, and we die at an appointed time. God ordained both. The psalmist writes: "You saw me before I was born. Every day of my life was recorded in your book. Every moment was laid out before a single day had passed" (139:16). All live in the time of God's choosing, and no one will die one moment before that which God has ordained.

This allotment of time that has been granted to every person represents their opportunity to reveal what lies hidden within their heart. Their heart will determine how they approach life and God's offer of eternal life. If their heart is dark, they will spend their lives doing that which is hurtful and destructive. They will bring heartbreak to themselves and others. Those who are evil will do their best work in the darkness because they prefer the darkness more than the light (John 3:19). On the other hand, others will bring gladness and joy to the people around them, and bystanders will observe the good they see and say, "That is a good person!" Over time many will be compelled to acknowledge the goodness they see.

In contrast, evil people will not be given that honorable compliment. So, those who fail to hear positive accolades will be forced to self-ascribe those accolades to themselves: "I'm a good person." If others are not quick to endorse this self-ascribed accolade, the accolade will be repeated with more desperation: "I'm a good person!" But this lie will fall short of its intended goal. Self-accolades are a desperate attempt to hide from the ugly truth and deny the reality of their dark, evil heart. Obviously, self-declarations of goodness are a mockery of the truth. And the evil person will fail in their attempt to adorn themselves with the clothing of the righteous.

Both those with good hearts and those with bad hearts will be unable to hide their true condition. Time will expose everyone, revealing their true nature. Everyone will either add to life or they will take away from life. Everyone will either be a source of encouragement and life or they will be a life-choking source of discouragement. In the proper season, every tree will yield its fruit and, in so doing, the tree can be easily identified. It cannot hide its true identity. This same principle can also be applied to people. As we read in Matthew: "Yes, the way to identify a tree or a person is by the kind of fruit that is produced" (7:20). There will be no doubt as to what is hidden in each person's heart. Time will have the power to reveal whether there is light or darkness within the heart. The final destiny of every person will have been written on every page of their life's story. Their final destiny will not be a mystery; it will not be hidden and only revealed at the last second with no time to change. No one will be able to say, "But I didn't know!" Each person who does not reveal the presence of Christ in his or her life will reveal the absence of Christ. There is no mystery in this fact. The type of life we live points toward our final destiny.

Each person will be rewarded based upon what they believe, and what a person truly believes will be reflect in what they do. Some will be resurrected to eternal life and others will be resurrected only to face the second death.

> I saw the dead, both great and small, standing before God's throne. And the books were opened, including the Book of Life. And the dead were judged according to the things written in the books, according to what they had done. The sea gave up the dead in it, and death and the grave gave up the dead in them. They were all judged

according to their deeds. And death and the grave were thrown into the lake of fire. This is the second death—the lake of fire. And anyone whose name was not found recorded in the Book of Life was thrown into the lake of fire. (Revelation 20:12–15)

Again, each person is allotted an amount of time. Time has the power to reveal our true identity, and that revelation is a gift from God, but we must be willing to look at what is revealed. Each person must be willing to look at the evidence God provides, or it will do no good. Honest introspection is needed. Questions need to be asked and truthfully answered. *What have I done with my life? How has my life helped others? Does my life portray the reality and truth of Christ? What am I?* Yes. God has given each of us the freedom to choose how we will live our lives, but he has also given us the ability to read our own record. Do not waste this gift.

And, undeniably, each choice we make comes with its own set of rewards and/or consequences. For example, we all have the freedom to step out in front of an 18-wheeler, but the consequences would be catastrophic. In like manner, we all have a choice regarding Christ. We can reject him, or we can accept his eternal gift. If we reject him, there are eternal consequences to our choice. Without Christ, a death sentence continues to loom in the future, but, with his blood applied, the sentence of death is commuted. And the righteous judgment of God has been met. Forgiveness stands in the place of condemnation. Romans tells us: "For the wages of sin is death, but the free gift of God is eternal life through Christ Jesus our Lord" (6:23).

Therefore, each person determines their own resurrection. God has given everyone the opportunity to choose their final destiny.

For if you confess with your mouth that Jesus is Lord and believe in your heart that God raised him from the dead, you will be saved. For it is by believing in your heart that you are made right with God, and it is by confessing with your mouth that you are saved. (Romans 10:9–11)

All who choose the way of sin and death will surely reap a crop of death, and all who choose the right path will reap a crop of life. And, during this course of time, God is not silent! His words ring out, admonishing those who do what is wrong, and encouraging those who do what is right. His instructions are simple and direct:

1. "He grants a treasure of good sense to the godly. He is their shield, protecting those who walk with integrity" (Proverbs 2:7).

2. He promises the upright that they will remain while assuring the wicked that they will be removed (Proverbs 2:21–22).

3. "Fear of the Lord is the beginning of knowledge. Only fools despise wisdom and discipline" (Proverbs 1:7).

4. "Happy is the person who finds wisdom and gains understanding" (Proverbs 3:13).

There should be no mistakes or lack of understanding in this area. There is a direct connection between the lives lived right now and eternity. Time will surely reveal the choice made by each person. Every second in life is a constant recommitment to a particular destiny—heaven or hell. And it must be remembered that God never intended for one human to wind up in hell—that was Satan's destiny (Wiese, 2017, p. 131).

Everyone will be judged whether they like it or not. With every passing moment our judgment draws nearer. It looms directly ahead. Those who choose right will see the face of God. The psalmist writes: "For the Lord is righteous, and he loves justice. Those who do what is right will see his face" (11:7). And those who choose a different path will not be allowed to stand in the presence of God (Psalm 5:4–6). They will be thrown into the place of torment prepared for Satan and his demons. The gates of hell will burst open in order to accommodate all who follow in Satan's footsteps, and all who do so must remember that the gates of hell only swing one way. All who enter will never reemerge. There will be no recovery from the second death. Christ will not come a second time to die (Hebrews 9:27–28). That is why God gives to each person a measure of time, and the time for salvation is now. The judgment of God is coming, and God will never negate his right to judge. Every person will be judged.

Without a doubt, it was never God's intention for anyone to be condemned. Hell was to be Satan's fate—not humanity's. It was Satan and his demons that rebelled in spite of holding onto a complete and personal understanding of God. They knew God! They had seen God. However, it was different for Adam and Eve. Their knowledge of God was much less. Yes. They sinned. They disobeyed God. There is no doubt that Adam and Eve had been warned by God, and for that reason Satan employed a measure of deception. Nevertheless, they sinned, and sin has but one outcome. The result of sin is death (Romans 6:23). Regardless of the circumstances, sin carries with it a penalty of death. A God of holiness will not tolerate sin. If an individual does not deal with their ungodliness before their death, God will deal with the ungodly person.

Our sin was great, but God's love was, and still is, greater. He did not withdraw himself from the world he had created. All of creation still bears his mark of glory and wonder. The apostle Paul writes: "From the time the world was created, people have seen the earth and sky and all that God made. They can clearly see his invisible qualities—his eternal power and divine nature" (Romans 1:20). We live in a world created out of love. Everyone who is willing to acknowledge this message displayed in creation knows that there is a God. In addition, there is the word of God—the Bible. The Bible provides additional instructions for those who want to know how to properly respond to the truth. Our need for Christ is clearly explained. Guidance for life is openly revealed. In addition, God has placed warnings in the Bible for all who struggle with doing that which is right. No one should be caught off guard by the final judgment. No one will have an excuse "for not knowing God" (Romans 1:20). God's love is present in life and on every page of the Bible. The Bible addresses the sinfulness of humanity, and it needs to be noted that the sinfulness of humanity has not been able to remove all of the traces of God's divine presence. God's love and truth are still here shaping our world.

Only You Can Choose

Again, Adam and Eve did sin, but they sinned without a full understanding of God. The evidence for this fact is clear. First, Adam and Eve lived in the world God created. Second, Adam and Eve interacted with God from within this created world. Third, Adam and Eve walked and spoke with God from within the garden where they had been placed (Genesis 3:8). It is plain to see that their understanding was limited to the earth; they had never seen the full glory of heaven. One might be willing to argue that Adam and Eve could not have fully understood the spiritual ramifications of their actions, but that still did not remove the impact of their sin. Nevertheless, because of Adam's sin, it became necessary for Christ to die to redeem humankind. Again, one might want to argue that we do not fully understand this most gracious act of Christ any more than the original sin. But, that does not reduce the importance of either one in the slightest degree. Both events occurred. Now, through Christ, humanity is given a second chance to live. Through Christ's sacrifice, sin and death have been stripped of their finality. The Bible clearly tells us that "the wages of sin is death, but the free gift of God is eternal life through Christ Jesus our Lord" (Romans 6:23).

God's plan is based upon grace. He has covered our spiritual debt himself. God came to Earth where humankind sinned. He took on the likeness of humanity. He emptied himself and took onto himself our limitations. He lived in the world he created. He submitted himself unto a cruel death. "And in human form he obediently humbled himself even further by dying a criminal's death on a cross" (Philippians 2:8). God dealt with the sin of humanity in an open and transparent manner. He measured the cost and paid the debt in full. The gift is free. "For God sent Jesus to take the punishment for our sins and to satisfy God's anger against us. We are made right with God when we believe that Jesus shed his blood, sacrificing his life for us" (Romans 3:25). Through Christ, humanity has a way to escape the consequences of sin.

There is no problem between humankind and God unless someone foolishly rejects Christ. "We are made right in God's sight when we trust in Jesus Christ to take away our sins. And we all can be saved in this same way, no matter who we are or what we have done" (Romans 6:22). It is that simple. However, the acceptance of God's free gift through Jesus Christ is a personal matter. No one can choose Christ on your behalf; each person must accept the free gift for themselves. God has made the provision; each person must make his or her own choice. In the end, the righteous will thank God throughout eternity while the unrighteous will raise their tortured voices to God throughout all eternity for not believing. Why anyone would choose to descend down into a devil's hell is beyond reasoning.

Unfortunately, many will stubbornly continue down the wrong path, rejecting God's plan. And the consequences for their ungodly choice will remain. Just as Satan and his demons chose a course of rebellion, all who choose to follow in their footsteps will meet a demon's fate. Their hideous fate does not have to be yours. Satan could not overthrow God, and neither can humanity. Rebellion will be crushed. You are not a fallen angel; you do not have to share their fate. However, anyone who dies in their sin will perish. Anyone who refuses to be separated from their sin has chosen death over life. "There is only one God, and there is only one way of being accepted by him. He makes people right with himself only by faith, whether they be Jews or Gentiles" (Romans 3:30).

Subsequently, there is only one choice in all of life that must be addressed, and that one choice carries eternal consequences: *Do I accept Christ, or do I reject him?* This crossroad will be encountered by everyone who draws breath, and Christ stands in the middle of that crossroad. It is a matter of life and death, and it cannot be avoided. Eternity hangs in the balance just as Christ hung upon the cross.

Did Christ die for you or not? Do you find a provision in his sacrifice for you? If not, then you are already dead, and the second death awaits you. Reading this book may be one of the last things you will ever do. However, if you accept his death as the atonement of your sin, you will inherit the life Christ laid down for you. Life and death rest within the power of your tongue. You will either speak words of life over yourself, or you will allow those words of life to remain missing. Regardless of what you may think, regardless of what your opinion may be, regardless of your feelings on the matter, God's plan will not be altered. You will come to God on his terms or you will not come at all.

It is time for you to make a decision. What do you choose? It is important to note that none of us are guaranteed tomorrow. We may not even make it through this day. Your decision is important. Humility can save your soul; it has the potential to touch the heart of God. God's plan for you is grace and mercy, but your time could be running out. "Grace is the help human beings receive from God on their voyage through earthly life. But once that voyage comes to an end, there is no more help from God" (DeStefano, 2020, p. 36). *Will you join Satan and his hoard of demons? Will you persist in holding God at bay?* There is no need to join Satan, and there is no reason to hold God off.

Contrary to what some might claim, no one will want to leave God's presence. His beauty, his wonder, and his splendor will captivate the heart and imagination of even the condemned. They will realize too late that they made a terrible mistake. No one will want to forfeit eternal life. Even in the face of God's great wrath, his eternal power and glory will shine forth. The Son of God will be highly exalted "so that at the name of Jesus every knee will bow, in heaven and on earth and under the earth, and every tongue will confess that Jesus Christ is Lord, to the glory of God the Father" (Philippians 2:10–11). His greatness will compel all to acknowledge him. Knees will automatically bend, but, for some, the acknowledgment will be limited. He will be their conquering king and not their savior. They will be the ones who would not bend their knees and acknowledge their great need for forgiveness. They will begin to cry out like the demons, fearing the coming judgment. The unforgiven will join Satan and his demons. They will join in the fate of the "cast-out ones." Woe unto them!

One can either stubbornly continue to claim their membership on death row or repent. The opportunity to repent remains as long as you have one more breath to breathe. Until that last breath arrives, love, grace, and mercy have the power to speak. They have the power to save, but once death speaks, all is lost. The condemned will have no hope. The unbeliever will have silenced love, grace, and mercy, and the gates of Satan's hell will open like a gigantic mouth to swallow one more lost soul. The blame for this will fall upon the unrepented person. No one will be able to cast the blame onto God because he sent his Son to die that all might live. The gift of Christ is not something that should be marginalized, scorned, or rejected. In him is life. Those who have done right will be present to watch the wicked breathe their last breath of unscorched air. Then the wicked will begin their eternal journey all alone; there will be no one to hold their hand as they transition into the second death.

Obviously, God's love can be rejected just like anyone else's love can be rejected. We all have the power to refuse another's love, but that refusal does not negate the love offered. The Father already proved his love when he sent his Son to die in our place. The Son proved his love when he willingly laid down his life, and the Holy Spirit proves his love every day when he brings the convicting power of God upon the hearts of those who do not believe in Christ. No matter how many times the Holy Spirit is rejected, he remains faithful. "And when he comes, he will convince the world of its sin, and of God's righteousness, and of the coming judgment" (John 16:8).

God will continue to bring his convicting power upon the world until the last day. Then the convicting power of God will end, and his judgment will descend because "a good judge must carry out justice" (Wiese, 2017, p. 74).

God is willing to be identified with those who were willing to be identified with him. By comparison, those who reject him during their lifetime will be rejected by him (Matthew 10:32). God will not attempt to maintain a relationship that never existed in the first place. God has every intention of abandoning the dead.

In the long run, God's Word will be proven right. Remember that God is not subject to time; he is beyond time, and he can afford to wait. He who is outside of time need not hurry. You, on the other hand, do need to examine your fate—you do need to be concerned. You can't afford to waste one more moment!

> The Lord Almighty says, "The day of judgment is coming, burning like a furnace. The arrogant and the wicked will be burned up like straw on that day. They will be consumed like a tree—roots and all. But for you who fear

my name, the Sun of Righteousness will rise with healing in his wings. And you will go free, leaping with joy like calves let out to pasture." (Malachi 4:1–2)

One can confidently commit his or her soul to God for safekeeping, but woe to the ones who cast God out now for they will surely be cast out later. You have been warned. Don't persist in foolishness. The psalmist says: "Only fools say in their hearts, 'There is no God'" (14:1). And, if you do not consider yourself to be foolish, there is only one course open to you. If God is, you have an obligation to search him out. Today is the day of salvation (2 Corinthians 6:2).

CHAPTER 6

The Resurrection of Life

MANY YEARS AGO, I was studying the concept of sin. I had already invested hundreds of hours into the project, and it was obvious that gaining a complete understanding of sin would be a daunting task without an end. Obtaining a comprehensive understanding of sin was the equivalent of entering into a bottomless pit with the intention of measuring the pit's greatest depth.

The more I studied the more I realized that humankind could never stand before the onslaught of sin. Sin was too complex, too diverse, and too cunning. We were simply outmatched. Everyone was well within its deadly range; its multifaceted assault would always be overwhelming. It could strike out at us from any number of unimaginable angles. Basically, sin had no equal. No one on Earth would stand before it; all would fall. Everyone would eventually succumb to its aggressive unending battering.

It was for this reason that God sent his Son into the world; Jesus would intervene. The Son of God would square off with evil. Jesus would come to Earth to conquer the unconquerable. The cost would be high, but the Son of God was willing to suffer in our place. He was willing to bleed for us, and he was willing to die a cruel death for us. Jesus would do all of this for us and reveal that. "Calvary is the supreme demonstration of Divine love" (Pink, 2006, p. 103). Then it would be Satan and his legions of demons that needed to fear. The righteousness of God would conquer our greatest foe. Sin would meet its match, and freedom from sin and death would follow in Jesus' footsteps.

Knowing that Jesus had conquered sin, I stopped and I prayed: "O Lord, I could study sin for the rest of my life, and I still would not learn all there is to know about this topic. In light of this fact, would you give me a complete understanding of sin so I can move on to something else?" I wanted to move on to something more refreshing and uplifting. The topic of sin was interesting, but it was also an unstoppable ugly foe. It was beginning to be a terribly disheartening subject.

Suddenly, to my amazement, God graciously and immediately answered my prayer. He responded by saying: "You are not capable of handling a complete understanding of sin." Following God's reply was a short, but deafening, silence. A few seconds went by before I realized that I was angry. After all, I did not ask if I had the ability to handle a complete understanding of sin. I asked for a complete understanding of sin. To me those two things were separate issues. I did not ask God to evaluate my abilities. I asked God for a complete understanding of the concept of sin! And I knew what I wanted!

As I continued to sit in my study, I genuinely began to comprehend just how far out of line I was with God. I was angry with him. A worm was unwittingly attempting to provoke a fight with an elephant. The insanity of my response to God's answer began to become more and more apparent with every

The Resurrection of Life

passing moment. I could do nothing but confess my sin to God. Why not? God already knew my sinful response to his gracious answer. God could have totally ignored my request. He didn't even have to answer at all. I was embarrassed and humiliated, and I wanted to come clean before God. So I confessed my sin and asked God for his forgiveness. After a few more moments passed by, I knew God's grace was covering my thoughts and my inappropriate attitude. I was graciously forgiven, but I still had a problem. I still wanted an answer to *my* original question. I was not content with being forgiven for my rudeness; I still found myself contemplating pushing the issue with God. I still wanted a complete understanding of sin. However, this time, I needed to incorporate more reverence into my push to know more.

Therefore, with a fresh coat of forgiveness covering me, I humbly pushed my original request back before God. I know: Some of you are questioning my humility and sincerity before God, but I was being honest and respectful. So, I humbly asked again: "O God would you give me a complete understanding of sin so I can move onto something else?" I lowered my head even as the words left my mouth. I was deeply concerned over the backlash that could follow. My head was lowered, and I was cringing a little. I did not want to provoke God, but I still wanted my request honored. Unfortunately, there was nothing but silence in the room. I slowly raised my head and looked around the room. I was wondering if God would answer, and if he did, what kind of a response he might provide.

Suddenly, a door began to appear. It almost appeared to be coming out of a mist. I looked intently at the door and wondered what it meant. Why was I seeing a door? It was a solid gray color but, otherwise, it had no defining characteristics or qualities other than I could not see what might lie on the other side. As I was contemplating the possible meaning of a door, it began to open. My eyes immediately focused upon the light that began to appear. The door only opened a fraction of an inch, just enough to break the seal along the leading edge of the door and a little at the top and bottom of the door. Anyone looking at the door would have said that the door was 99.99 percent closed.

Nevertheless, the light that came through the leading edge of the door and around the top and at the bottom of the door was incredibly brilliant and bright white. It was so white that I immediately knew it had to be the source of all light, but the whiteness and the brilliance of the light was not the only thing captivating my attention. This pure white light was completely different; every particle of light was infused with content. The thoughts of God were embedded within every particle. The knowledge of God was brilliant. His thoughts and his light were one! They shared a oneness I had never contemplated before. I knew from the Scriptures that God was light (John 8:12), and I knew that God was omniscient, but this was spectacular.

I already understood that God the Father, God the Son, and God the Holy Spirit shared a state of oneness, but I never entertained any concept that there might be a state of oneness among the different attributes of God. That realization was shocking! This unity was divinely brilliant! Just to have experienced this incredibly small, fractional view of God's light and mind was breathtaking. I sat there in absolute awe and wonder. I was speechless. When you are shown something that is beyond description, when you are shown something that words cannot touch, one has no words. It was the most beautiful thing I had ever experienced. It exceeded my wildest expectations. Even now, I find myself struggling to describe the wonder and the beauty of the experience. Words fall short when trying to describe God's glory. I never knew thoughts could be seen, and light could be comprehended. God's thoughts weren't written on paper; they were unified and displayed within this magnificently glorious light. God's thoughts on that day were not audible. I saw them! I saw God's wisdom splendidly displayed. It was a blending of art and wisdom. And I was just seeing a fractional view of just

The Resurrection of Life

two of God's attributes. What unimaginable beauty lies ahead for the redeemed? With this event in my mind, I cannot imagine what the future holds for the redeemed.

God's wisdom can be found throughout the Bible; his wisdom is transcendent, knowing no barriers. No man can confound it. No language can contain it, and time cannot stop it. And humans would do well to acknowledge him. I know that we do not fully comprehend God. We have had the Bible for hundreds of years, and, yet, we still do not comprehend it all. It still offers us mysteries and diversities that cause us to stumble, but that does not change its message. "In spite of its diversity, the Bible presents a single unfolding story: God's redemption of human beings" (McDowell, 1999, p. 6). Everyone would do well to read the Bible. It has the power to open every eye. God has the power to illuminate the understanding (Proverbs 9:10).

Moments passed by before I realized I was allowing hundreds of godly thoughts to rush past me without any attempt on my part to retain them. In a panic I grabbed the next three thoughts that came rushing into my study. Those three thoughts were going to be mine; I was not going to leave this encounter with God empty-handed. I held onto them while I continued to look at the stream of light and thoughts that continued pouring into the room. It was so captivating. I was paralyzed by the sheer beauty. God had my undivided attention. I could have sat surrounded by the thoughts of God for the rest of my life, and I would have never gotten bored.

Moments later, to my horror I noticed that the three thoughts I intended to keep were gone. They had vanished! They had been washed away by the hundreds of thoughts still pouring into the room. Panic-stricken, I grabbed the next two thoughts that came streaming toward me. I was determined to hold onto them. So I pictured myself clutching them to my chest. I did not want them to be washed away like the first three. Unfortunately, seconds later they were gone. In desperation I lunged for the next thought that came toward me. It was mine; I bent over holding it close to my chest. I did not want to leave this encounter empty-handed. I tried to block out the rest of the light and its content as it streamed into the room, but it was not to be! Despite my valiant efforts, that one thought was washed away in a matter of seconds. The content pouring into the room far exceeded my capacity; I was powerless to retain a single thought. I began to fear that I would leave this beautiful engagement with God with nothing to show for it, and it was the experience of a lifetime.

Now came the most shocking part of this beautiful event. Not only did I fail to retain one of God's thoughts, but now I realized that I would not leave this encounter with my life. The whole thing was proving to be too much. My physical body was overloaded. I was unable to handle this tiny fractional view of God's holiness. My death was imminent! My body and my mind were slipping away. I had been so focused on retaining God's thoughts that I failed to notice the danger I was in until it was too late.

Powerless to save my own life I needed God to intervene. Yet, despite my need for help, I could not get my body to respond. I attempted to call out to him, but nothing worked. No words came out of my mouth. I couldn't even make a desperate sound. I started accepting the fact that I would die. Nevertheless, the experience had been a pleasure and a privilege. These moments had revealed a small hint of what was in store for the redeemed.

Heaven would truly be heaven. I had known that heaven would be a land far beyond anyone's imagination, but this experience hinted at the level of grandeur far beyond imagining. God was far more than the mind could conceive; an all-encompassing beauty was lying ahead for the redeemed. The beauty and the pleasures of this life are as sawdust compared to eternity with God. God will join with us in some way where every particle of our mind, soul, and body will be illuminated by his Spirit, creating an indescribable spiritual unity.

All of a sudden the light around the door grabbed my attention. It had started to change. At first the change was most noticeable at the top and at the bottom of the door. As God began to close the door, the light started tapering back at the top and at the bottom of the door; it was moving away from where the hinges were located. It was retreating farther and farther toward the leading edge of the door. Darkness was creeping across the gap at the top and bottom. I was elated! I had a glimmer of hope that I might not die. I tried to scream for God to hurry. I desperately needed God to realize that I had reached my limits. My death was imminent. Hurry!

Although, I knew that the door needed to close at a faster rate, God never increased the speed. The receding light at the top and bottom never quickened. God seemed indifferent to my plight, but in reality, he was indifferent to my evaluation of my plight; he had his own pace, and it wasn't going to change just because I knew it needed too. Everything was progressing according to God's timing, and he was not interested in my opinion. My desperation did not move him in the slightest degree. In fact, I never realized that a door opened so little could take so long to close. I was shocked and exasperated with God's turtle-like speed. Really! No one would ever need to tell me that God created the slow-moving turtle. I was forced to wait for God to do his thing, and he was not in any hurry. The door would close in God's good timing regardless of my efforts to speed him up. God seemed to be totally disinterested, apathetic to my input.

I later realized that, first, God's turtle-like speed in closing the door was his mild rebuke. After all, I had disregarded his word when he told me that I did not have the capacity to handle a complete understanding of sin. God attempted to warn me, and I shrugged his warning off. Second, He, not I, had the greater understanding of the enormity, the complexity, and the depravity of sin. A total understanding of sin was beyond my comprehension. Just as a child is unable to comprehend the mind of his or her parent, neither can we comprehend the mind of God. Third, I should have trusted God. He truly understood the mental capacity needed to handle a complete understanding of sin, and I did not have such a capacity. And, finally, God was administering a mild form of discipline cloaked in humor, grace, and patience. I was never actually in danger. God was controlling the content coming into the room, he was shielding me the whole time, and he determined the length of the exposure. I was completely in his hand every second. The Lord's gentle hand kept me safe as he increased my capacity to understand and trust him. God was in charge, and he still is. The resurrection will unfold just as he had planned. It will not be one moment too soon or one moment too late, and our opinion on the matter will not change one fraction of God's plan.

When I look back upon this encounter, I realize that many things changed. My concept of God changed. He is now more! I now experientially realized just how much he is in control. He is amazingly diverse, intelligent, powerful, and, yet, compassionate. He is willing to enlighten anyone truly searching for truth and understanding. We just need to listen. I could not have imagined his beauty, his unmeasurable depth, or his wonder and awe. No one but God could combine light and mental concepts into one thing. And the true complexity of God is yet to be revealed. And, yes! His humor must be unmeasurable as well. I know he was having a little fun at my expense, but I have to admit that I had it coming. If I was struck speechless by a fractional view of the oneness shared between just two of God's attributes, how much more will the redeemed be paralyzed by the unbridled glory of God? In their new resurrected bodies the redeemed will be able to stand in the holy presence of God Almighty. A fractional view of God will not be necessary. They will see him face-to-face.

> Now we see things imperfectly as in a poor mirror, but then we will see everything with perfectly clarity. All

that I know now is partial and incomplete, but then I will know everything completely, just as God knows me now. (1 Corinthians 13:12)

The Transcendent Nature and Power of God

The redeemed will experience the fullness of God. They will see what no eye has seen, they will hear what no ear has ever heard, and they will comprehend what no mind has ever imagined (1 Corinthians 2:9). The redeemed will see, hear, and experience God's unmeasurable loving forgiveness, grace, mercy, longsuffering, kindness, goodness, faithfulness, patience, joy, truthfulness, and justice. His holiness and purity will impregnate every aspect of life. His omnipresence, his omnipotence, and his omniscience will maintain the eternal peace that will bind all life into him. The redeemed will be literally in God and God in them (John 14:20). Friendship with God will be the norm. The redeemed will see the one who was willing to take on the likeness of man and die that they might live. Eternal life will be God's gift to anyone wise enough and humble enough to accept it.

Every attribute, every characteristic, every quality of God will be experienced by the redeemed in a state of oneness which will exponentially magnify each and every component of God and the quality of eternal life. This intensified life to come will have a depth, a width, and a height that cannot be compared to anything currently experienced. The eternal beauty of God simply does not exist in our realm. But, one day, the redeemed will experience all of God in a unified, bonded, fused state. God's oneness will cause every aspect of life to be amplified into an indescribable beautiful experience. In my extremely limited fractional view of God's light and knowledge, the light of God was intensified by being infused with knowledge, and the knowledge of God was illuminated by the light. Even though I experienced the light and knowledge of God, I cannot begin to imagine God in his fullness. I only know that we will never get bored with exploring God's divine nature.

Next, I would like to elaborate upon the power exhibited by the light and knowledge of God as it poured into my study. It was unique; it knew no limits or restrictions. It needed no permission. The light came into the room unhindered; it passed straight though my body as if my body wasn't even there. My body didn't even slow it down. Yet, it didn't hurt me in any way. The flow was steady and consistent; it had the power to fill the room and to continue on its way. It produced an immediate and profound effect upon me. It changed my understanding of God and his written Word. The experience illuminated certain passages in the Bible; those passages took on a whole new meaning. The Bible now had a greater depth and richness than ever before.

Particular passages flashed through my mind after the event, but now they were alive. They carried a greater complexity and simplicity at the same time. One such verse is in the Gospel of John: "That evening on the first day of the week, the disciples were meeting behind locked doors because they were afraid of the Jewish leaders. Suddenly, Jesus was standing there among them!" (John 20:19). I knew from reading this passage that Jesus could appear anywhere he pleased; he was not limited or hindered by physical restraints like locked doors. He was free to move about in our material world independent of the natural laws governing everyone else.

His many demonstrations of his supernatural abilities were a hint of what was to come for all those who love and trust him now. However, I never conceptualized the transcendent nature and power of God as I should have. He is above the natural laws of nature; he knows no restrictions. He can circumvent his natural laws at any time of his choosing (McGrath, 2011, p. 98). He was and is supreme and unsurpassable, and the redeemed will follow Jesus into this supernatural world. That means the supernatural or divine nature of God's world will become the norm for the redeemed. Their new world will greatly surpass this current natural world with all of its limitations and restrictions. Thousands of things will change in an instant. The redeemed will see the blending of the natural and the supernatural just as Jesus was the perfect blending of humanity and divinity.

> Eight days later the disciples were together again, and this time Thomas was with them. The doors were locked; but suddenly, as before, Jesus was standing among them. He said, "Peace be with you." Then he said to Thomas, "Put your finger here and see my hands. Put your hand into the wound in my side. Don't be faithless any longer. Believe!" "My Lord and my God!" Thomas exclaimed. (John 20:26–28)

Once again Jesus entered the room where the disciples were gathered. Locked doors posed no problem for him, but this time was different. Jesus made sure that Thomas was present. On Jesus' prior visit Thomas had not been there. When the other disciples told Thomas that they had seen Jesus, Thomas did not believe them. In fact, Thomas insisted on proof! He wanted to put his fingers into the wounds in Jesus' hands and thrust his hand into the wound in Jesus' side before he would believe (John 20:24–25).

Nevertheless, upon Jesus' return, Jesus was willing to furnish the proof. The risen Savior had heard Thomas's demand for proof. Jesus was clearly demonstrating his omnipresence. In fact, Jesus was demonstrating the omnipresence, omnipotence, and the omniscience of a risen Savior. This demonstration of divinity will be the norm in the coming world of the redeemed. God's presence, God's power, and God's all-knowing nature will be the dwelling place of the redeemed. Like Thomas, the redeemed will also encounter the grace, the kindness, and the patience of a loving God. This will be the norm in the world to come.

Unquestionably, there is one point that needs to be stressed in this encounter between Thomas and Jesus. Jesus was demonstrating that there is nothing spoken that God does not hear. God hears all! Every word of doubt, every word of hate, and every malicious word spoken in secret will be made known. In fact, it is already known by God the moment it is spoken. As Paul writes: "The day will surely come when God, by Jesus Christ, will judge everyone's secret life" (Romans 2:16). And according to Luke there will be no exemptions. "For everything that is hidden or secret will eventually be brought to light and made plain to all" (Luke 8:17). Every word spoken in secret is spoken into the ear of God. This means that you and I will hear every word we ever spoke played back for us on the Day of Judgment. The redeemed will not escape this quickly approaching day of accounting, nor will the damned escape their approaching judgment. However, there will be several notable differences between what the redeemed experience and what the damned experience. The redeemed will hear everything played back under grace because they have already passed from death into life (John 3:35–36, 6:47).

First, the redeemed are covered by the blood of Christ, and, therefore, they will not see eternal damnation. They are the forgiven, but they will suffer the potential loss for their sinful thoughts, words, and actions. In light of the coming judgment, the redeemed should strive to live within God's character and nature. If God does not condone something, leave it alone. If God commands something, do it. The redeemed should live as though God was standing right beside them, and, therefore, they should avoid speaking evil of one another. The apostle Paul asks an important question: "So why do you condemn another Christian? Why do you look down on another Christian?

Remember, each of us will stand personally before the judgment seat of God" (Romans 14:10).

Jesus came to save—not to condemn—and those who have placed their souls in his safekeeping are not under condemnation. Therefore, stop condemning one another. The redeemed must live life in a manner worthy of Christ's work. Spend your time imitating his life. Live life in the light of God and you will find yourselves catching glimpses of what is to come. Obedient believers will not be caught off guard when their Lord returns. All of the redeemed should strive to hear these words: "Well done; you lived your life in a way that honored me" (Matthew 25:14–30).

The second difference between the redeemed and the damned is their life on this earth. The redeemed should find themselves living in a physical world while preparing for the one to come. The damned should realize that they are living and investing into a world that will pass away. Notably, the redeemed are living at the lowest point they will ever know while the damned are living at the highest point they will ever attain. The redeemed choose to die daily to this world in their pursuit of God while the damned choose to live now and die later. The redeemed are willing to give up now that they might gain far more in God's kingdom. The damned refuse to let go, attempting to save their lives only to lose everything in the end (Matthew 16:25). One lives with eternity in sight while the other discounts the supernatural. One lives for the long haul while the other is in it for the short run. The redeemed search for what cannot be lost while the damned hold on to what will perish. The redeemed have a vision for the future. In contrast, the damned perish because they have no vision (Proverbs 29:18). There are two different pathways: one leading toward life while the other is nothing more than a dead-end.

The third difference between the redeemed and the damned is the fact that the redeemed have already started living the eternal life (John 5:24). This temporal life is but a training ground for the redeemed. Their progressively spiritual depth and understanding directly depend upon how seriously they handle God's directions for their life. The more they invest themselves into God's kingdom, the more of him they experience. Whereas, the dead have already failed to live; they have chosen to remain under a death sentence (John 3:18). The dead have rejected life; however, the stark reality of their decision has not been fully realized yet.

Currently, the redeemed see "things imperfectly as in a dim mirror, but then we will see everything with perfect clarity. All that I know now is partial and incomplete, but then I will know everything completely, just as God knows me now" (1 Corinthians 13:12). I can attest to the reality Paul spoke about from my own incredibly small fractional view of God's light and thoughts. The "clarity" was perfect; the beauty of God was inconceivable, completely contrary to what one might have anticipated. Nothing could be more tragically pathetic than to have lived and died without constructively coming to terms with the reality of Jesus Christ. Not believing in him does not make him any less true or any less real. Truth doesn't need my endorsement any more than it needs your endorsement. Truth stands independent of humanity. As it was mentioned above, the redeemed will one day see God with "perfect clarity." God's love for the redeemed is so complete that he allows them "to be called his children" (1 John 3:1).

> Yes, dear friends, we are already God's children, and we can't even imagine what we will be like when Christ returns. But we do know that when he comes we will be like him, for we will see him as he really is. And all who believe this will keep themselves pure, just as Christ is pure. (1 John 3:2–3)

It is true. The redeemed are the children of God regardless of all their flaws, shortcomings, and sin. They have been separated from their sin by the blood of Jesus Christ, and they will be like him upon his return. The verses above make this fact plain and simple. The author, Pink, further elaborates by saying: "How blessed to know that the great and holy God loved his people before heaven and earth were called into existence, that he had set his heart upon them from all eternity" (2006, p. 100).

The redeemed have already started out on an eternal adventure that will culminate in them meeting Jesus face to face. The eternal Son of God will not only be their Savior, but their older brother, friend, and companion (John 15:14–15, Acts 5:30–31, 2 Timothy 1:9–10). He is the bridegroom and we are the bride (Isaiah 62:5, Matthew 25:1). We will forever be united with the source of all life. Therefore, it is time to start trusting the heavenly Father. Some readers may find this concept difficult to embrace because their earthly fathers were less than loving, but that doesn't make it any less true. Was your childhood stolen from you? Well, here is your chance to know what a Father can really be like. Learn to trust; learn to rely upon him. All who lost their childhood are offered an opportunity to know the love of a father.

God's plan can be trusted. His plan will come to fruition. The redeemed will not be abandoned. On the contrary, the redeemed have been left here in Jesus' name in order to carry on with God's ongoing mission of reconciliation. What Jesus began so many years ago is still being carried out today. The redeemed are God's witnesses to those who are determined to perish. However, the redeemed do need to do a better job of portraying the love of God. We need to stop living so far beneath our divine calling. The hope within us must be openly shared. Our living testimony in many cases is too weak; it needs to be empowered by holy living. The resurrection power of God is within the redeemed. The Scriptures declare that the believers need to draw near to

God and he will draw near to them (James 4: 8–10, Hebrews 10:19–23). Allow the world to see God through your life. Live in the presence and in the power of God.

God's Glory Revealed, but Not Seen

Moses, a prominent figure in the Old Testament, experienced many ups and downs throughout his life. He was eventually raised up by God to lead the budding nation of Israel out of their bondage in the land of Egypt. On one occasion, Moses asked God: "Please let me see your glorious presence" (Exodus 33:18). What a bold move and what a splendid request. Who wouldn't want to see God, and experience the mighty presence of God? But the Lord God told Moses, "you may not look directly at my face, for no one may see me and live" (Exodus 33:20). God knew that his holy presence was too much for Moses, and it would have consumed him in an instant. Just as darkness cannot stand in the presence of light, neither can the sinful flesh stand in the presence of that which is holy. Light consumes darkness just as surely as the holiness of God would consume sinful flesh. Until we have been resurrected into our new glorified bodies, we cannot stand in the presence of God without some form of divine intervention or protection. This fact becomes all too apparent through God's response to Moses.

> The Lord continued, "Stand here on this rock beside me. As my glorious presence passes by, I will put you in the cleft of the rock and cover you with my hand until I have passed. Then I will remove my hand, and you will see me from behind. But my face will not be seen." (Exodus 33:21–23)

God granted Moses's request up to the point that his physical body could endure. The following day, Moses went back up Mount Sinai to meet with the Lord as he had been instructed

The Resurrection of Life

(Exodus 34:2). "Moses was up on the mountain with the L[ord] forty days and forty nights . . . When Moses came down [the] mountain . . . he wasn't aware that his face glowed" (Exc[dus] 34:28–29). Moses was powerfully affected by his encounter [with] God. The change in his facial appearance only hinted towar[d the] inward changes. His mind, his thoughts, and his emotions [had] been touched by God. Moses received a foretaste of what [the] redeemed will experience for all eternity.

The redeemed will know God's deep passion and commitm[ent] toward Israel and to all who have been faithful. It will be m[ore] than an intellectual encounter; it will be a deep relati[onal] exchange. Moses was changed forever. This was a divi[ne,] intimate experience surpassing the physical intimacy betw[een] that of a man and a woman. Moses's face literally lit up, glow[ing] from his encounter with God. What Moses experienced f[or a] short time will be the norm for the redeemed. There will b[e no] end to standing in God's glory; there will be no holding bac[k on] the part of God.

We should not be surprised by the changes in Moses's b[od]y. The spiritual, transcendent realm is powerful, leaving be[hind] physical tangible evidence upon those who have encount[ered] God. Moses's physical body simply recorded the di[vin]e interaction between him and God. Divine power will al[way]s leave its signature behind, but this really shouldn't be stun[nin]g news. Years ago, when I was in some of my psychology cla[ss]es, we discussed the differences in the physiological functio[nin]g between the brains of criminals and the brains of the ave[rag]e person.

Our modern society observed these differences [an]d incorrectly assumed that the criminal mind was made differe[nt]ly and, therefore, they were not fully accountable for their crim[in]al behavior. I spoke with a Christian judge who held this appa[llin]g view. In essence, he was blaming God! If he would have follo[we]d his logic far enough, he would have realized that he was ma[kin]g criminal behavior God's fault. Wrong! That was and is a false assumption. The physical differences in the criminal brain versus the average person are merely evidences of how much time the criminal has spent in the presence of evil. Surely, people are not foolish enough to think that only divine power leaves behind its calling card. Demonic power leaves its mark behind as well. And, in essence, the difference in the criminal's brain versus the average person's brain should be looked upon as evidence against the criminal. This kind of evidence should be just as damning as a knife dripping with blood.

Another example of just how different it will be for the redeemed in the age to come can be observed in the New Testament. The Book of Acts records the events between Stephen, a believer in Jesus Christ, and the Sanhedrin, the religious ruling body of the Jewish nation. Stephen was arrested and brought before "the high council" (Acts 6:12). Before Stephen was given the opportunity to respond to the false charges brought against him, the attention of the entire high council was drawn toward him "because his face became as bright as an angel's [face]" (Acts 6:13–15). His glowing face was a biblical endorsement from God, attesting to the character of Stephen and the message he was about to deliver.

The Holy Spirit was making a clear connection between Stephen and Moses. Just as God's anointing had been noted upon Moses, so, it was now upon Stephen. They were both men of God, both led by and empowered by God. Both men knew God on an intimate level. God's endorsement of Stephen meant that the Sanhedrin needed to heed the testimony that was about to be delivered. To ignore, to marginalize, or to reject Stephen's testimony was to ignore, marginalize, or reject God. God was warning the Sanhedrin to proceed with caution. Stephen's message was God's message. Stephen had been brought before the Sanhedrin based upon unjust charges. Regardless of how things may have appeared to the Sanhedrin, "God will not be

The Resurrection of Life

unjust to himself. God shows mercy to the truly penitent, not to the impenitent (Luke 13:3). To continue in sin and reckon upon Divine mercy remitting punishment is diaboli (Pink, 2006, p. 96). The Sanhedrin should have pondered all of the evidence being presented to them. Stephen was to God's man. God illuminated Stephen's face for the benefi the Sanhedrin—not for Stephen's sake. Stephen wasn't stan in front of a mirror, he was standing in front of the Sanhec However, Stephen's illuminated face may serve as a hint as the faces of the redeemed may look when we all stand in eternal presence of God.

Stephen had but one goal as he stood before the high cou he would follow the Holy Spirit's leading no matter where might take him. The spiritual bond of intimacy between Step and God could not be broken. This becomes all too apparer we travel through the story. Stephen recounts the long his of Israel. His account drew attention to the great moment success and the terrible failures within Jewish history. Step pointed out how the high council was like the stubborn ances of old, being "heathen at heart and deaf to the truth" (7:51). According to Stephen, the high council was following ancient pattern of disobedience when they murdered Jesus Messiah (Acts 7:52).

At this point, it needs to be noted that throughout bib history God had continued to point out various sin individuals and groups so that they might have the opportu to repent, avoiding the judgment that would surely follow. unquestionably, this was the point of Stephen's discours this occasion. Stephen's testimony was God's warning to high council, but the Jewish leadership failed to turn tov repentance. Instead, the Jewish leadership was infuriated, they shook their fists in rage" (Acts 7:54).

This spiritually poor and threatening response from the council did not alter Stephen's discourse. Stephen would cont to follow the Holy Spirit. In fact, the high council's disobedience was about to clash with Stephen's obedience. With the Jewish leaders in a rage, poised to strike with deadly accuracy, the Holy Spirit continued leading Stephen down a path of confrontation. The Holy Spirit enabled Stephen to see what the others could not see. Stephen "gazed steadily upward into heaven and saw the glory of God, and he saw Jesus standing in the place of honor at God's right hand" (Acts 7:54–55).

At this point, Stephen had a choice. He could enjoy the beauty of the moment and stand in pure awe. This was a gift! He could have kept the moment private and lived, or he could share the moment and further enrage the high council. The choice was fully his. Would he stand in silence and live, or speak and die? The high council was enraged. They only needed one more comment from Stephen and violence would ensue. The Holy Spirit could see this; Stephen could see this.

Nevertheless, Stephen was not intimidated by the threatening mood. Stephen had but one goal: He would follow the leading of the Holy Spirit no matter where that might take him. He didn't fear the outcome. Stephen decided to share the moment by saying: "Look, I see the heavens opened and the Son of Man standing in the place of honor at God's right hand!" (Acts 7:56). He had shared this beautiful moment between himself and God. It was a gift from Stephen to them, but it was a gift they refused to receive.

The outcome came swiftly and violently. Stephen was dragged out of the city where he was immediately stoned to death (Act 7:57–58). This actually had no effect on Stephen's position. On Stephen's part, there was no running in fear; there was no effort from him to retaliate. In fact, the opposite occurred. Stephen prayed for his murderers (Acts 7:59–60). Full of the Holy Spirit, the world had no effect upon Stephen. He felt no need to return the stones back to their original owners at a high rate of speed. Instead, Stephen prayed. Stephen was obviously standing with one foot in the land of the redeemed. The coming glory outweighs the cost. He could see the Master of the Resurrection; he would not be lured away from his Lord. Truly, the redeemed will be firmly planted in the kingdom of God. Stephen was human. He wanted to live, but from his vantage point he could see into both worlds. Obviously, Stephen's desire to live in the supernatural realm overpowered his desire to remain in the physical world. The land of the redeemed was calling him home.

It is evident from all the outward visible signs in Stephen that he was caught up in a powerful, intimate, loving embrace from God Almighty. Stephen was so raptured by this loving embrace that he did not want anyone to miss out on what he was experiencing. Not even the high council—especially the high council. His current ongoing terrifying death had no power. His body was dying, but he wasn't. While being stoned to death, Stephen did not want even those stoning him to miss out on God's divine all-encompassing presence. Stephen was not overwhelmed by death. Life in God, life with God, was casting a shadow over death. Death had been cut down to size. Stephen found himself compelled to pray for his executioners: "'Lord Jesus, receive my spirit.' And he fell to his knees, shouting, 'Lord, don't charge them with this sin!' And with that he died" (Acts 7:59–60). Stephen's last moments on earth were used to pray so that no one need miss out on God. And all Christians, like Stephen, "have God-given assignments to complete during our brief stay on earth, even though we will soon be departing for our eternal home. Yet while we temporarily reside in this world, we are to guard against becoming entangled in it" (Jeffress, 2017, p. 223).

Stephen succeeded in completing his assignments. He exhibited the willingness to freely mix his blood with his message of Jesus Christ. He wanted his would-be murderers to know the gift of life found only through the blood of Christ. He met their anger with God's forgiveness. He met their hatred with God's love. He overcame their violence with God's peace. The high council had no power over Stephen. In other words, Stephen had firsthand experience with life's greatest challenge, and he could answer Paul's most perplexing question without any hesitation or reservation.

> Can anything ever separate us from Christ's love? Does it mean he no longer loves us if we have trouble or calamity, or are persecuted, or are hungry or cold or in danger or threatened with death? (Even the Scriptures say, "For your sake we are killed every day; we are being slaughtered like sheep.") No, despite all these things, overwhelming victory is ours through Christ, who loved us. And I am convinced that nothing can ever separate us from his love. Death can't, and life can't. The angels can't, and the demons can't. Our fears for today, our worries about tomorrow, and even the power of hell can't keep God's love away. Whether we are high above the sky or in the deepest ocean, nothing in all creation will ever be able to separate us from the love of God that is revealed in Christ Jesus our lord. (Romans 8:35–39)

Stephen answered Paul's question in front of this ruling body of Jewish leaders. They were given a beautiful gift—an insight into the heart of God. The only real question remaining was what they would do with the gift. Life's challenges do not separate us from God, they are designed to draw us nearer to him. God challenges everyone at different points in life—even the high council of Israel. Stephen had taken the time to point this very fact out to the high council moments before they murdered him. The Holy Spirit spoke through Stephen to remind the high council that God challenged Abraham (Acts 7:2–7). Then God rewarded Abraham for his obedience (Acts 7:8). God challenged Joseph (Acts 7:9). Then God walked with Joseph through the challenges placed before him (Acts 7:9–10). God challenged the land of Egypt and Canaan (Acts 7:11). Once again, God provided the answer to the challenge (Acts 7:12–15). Stephen continued with this recounting of Israel's many challenges and the results that followed right up to this present high council. Stephen was giving the high council a divine invitation to join with God. They, too, could peer into God's holy realm with Stephen.

Then Stephen delivered God's challenge for the high council, but evidently the high council failed to catch the pattern being presented to them. God, without fail, always presents the challenge. Then the one challenged must search and wait for the provision of God to appear. In this manner, the challenged can constructively meet the challenge with divine guidance. This is God's pattern; this is how God works with humankind. Challenges come so that the challenged might walk with God. God was and is always the provision. Slow down. Take note! This is God's call to you; this is God's invitation for you to walk with him and know him. This is God's divine pattern and answer to life. This is the God of the redeemed. Here, in this life, we are to learn how to walk by faith, not by our own natural sight (2 Corinthians 5:7). Don't focus on life! Focus on God. This is the pattern for the redeemed because this is how God has chosen to reveal himself. The redeemed will be led by God where true life can be found. Narrow is the road that leads to life and few ever find it (Matthew 7:14). God is not leading us through life; he is leading us into himself. He is the life that we are to discover.

Death Defying Joy

The high council was not the only one being challenged in those moments when Stephen stood before them. Stephen was facing his own set of challenges at the same time. In fact, he embraced his challenges so seamlessly that few ever noticed. First, Stephen had to be willing to be a part of the challenge being presented to the high council. If the high council handled the challenge poorly, Stephen would most likely die. He could see their anger building. When the high council had met their breaking point, God opened up heaven and Stephen could see his Savior standing next to the Father (Acts 8:55). It must have been a shocking contrast to see God the Father and God the Son in the midst of the angry Sanhedrin mob. Nevertheless, it was still up to Stephen as to whether or not he would share this moment with his angry listeners. Despite the ugliness of the situation, an exciting joy filled Stephen's heart. The author Randy Alcorn appears to have been right: "To see God will be our greatest joy, the joy by which all others will be measured" (2004, p. 172).

The question of sharing or holding back must have ripped straight through Stephen's brain: "Do I share this moment with the high council?" Stephen knew this would be the cap, the finishing touch, the last stroke of the paintbrush completing the challenge for the high council. If they handled the challenge correctly, Stephen would have gained some new brothers in Christ. The relationship between them would have been extremely close and forever unique. Nevertheless, Stephen knew he was on dangerous ground. Even still, he never hesitated. The final part of the high council's challenge had to be delivered regardless of the outcome. Second, Stephen had one goal: He would be obedient. He would speak freely. He knew his destiny; he knew where he would wind up if they failed God's challenge. He could not be separated from God's love. He was numbered among the redeemed.

In so doing, Stephen followed Jesus' example. He looked beyond the pain and the suffering. He could see his resurrected Savior. Stephen could see his eternal destiny among the redeemed, and his vision cleared the path ahead for him. He shared the vision given to him with the high council, but they were too shortsighted to benefit. They could not see that far ahead, and they were unwilling to hear the words of the Holy Spirit or the visual witness of the Holy Spirit in Stephen's glowing face. What the high council refused to see and hear would become a permanent loss; it would not reappear. There was really no mystery. It was all very simple. If a person isn't walking with God in this life, that person will not walk with God throughout eternity. Only those who actively walk with God now will find themselves participating in the resurrection of the redeemed. No one can live like hell and then think they will not find themselves in hell. The redeemed will see the face of God while the damned will behold the wrath of God. In the course of time, a soul-wrenching shudder will rip through their chest. Unlike Stephen, they will have no vision of a savior, they will not look beyond the pain and suffering, and they have no destiny.

On the other hand, the resurrection of the redeemed will be a place where loss will be unknown. The redeemed will be full, not empty. They will see what God has prepared for them.

> "Don't be troubled. You trust God, now trust in me. There are many rooms in my Father's home, and I am going to prepare a place for you. If this were not so, I would tell you plainly. When everything is ready, I will come and get you, so that you will always be with me where I am. And you know where I am going and how to get there." (John 14:1–4)

Jesus instructed the redeemed not to be troubled; they were to believe in him. As he was about to depart from this world, he wanted those who would follow in his footsteps to know that there were many rooms in his Father's kingdom, and that he was going to prepare a place for every believer. Upon their arrival, they would find a perfectly prepared place for them. These words were to be their vision for the future and their assurance for the present. No believer would feel out of place upon their arrival. Everyone had the assurance of the Son of God. They would dwell in the presence of God. But not all of Jesus' words were futuristic. Jesus also stated that after his resurrection, the Holy Spirit would live in the believer (John 14:17). Jesus said:

"When I am raised to life again, you will know that I am in my Father, and you are in me, and I am in you" (John 14:20).

In the Likeness of the Son

As we continue our search for an understanding of the land of the redeemed, we need to remember all that Jesus did. Many spiritual insights can be gleaned just from observing Jesus' ministry. When Jesus entered into our world, he took on the likeness of man (Romans 8:3). Jesus became like us. He shared not just our likeness, but also many of our limitations. He knew our circumstances, our weakness, and our temporal existence. In like manner, the redeemed will take on the likeness of the Son of God (Romans 6:5–8). We will become like him. We will learn of his unlimited being, his strength, and his eternal nature. He shared in our death, and we shall share in his life. Through looking at the uniqueness of Jesus throughout the gospels we can continue gaining a glimpse of how life might be for the redeemed.

First, there will be no thirst for life. There will be no chasing after the next life-giving thrill. The living waters Jesus offered will take "away thirst altogether" (John 4:14). Life will be a never-ending spring within each person, giving them eternal life (John 4:14). Life will be encountered from a state of fullness—not from a state of deprivation. Each moment, each hour, each day will be an opportunity to explore the vastness of God. Jesus spent each day looking to see where the Father was working. Once he saw the presence of his Father, he joined in (John 5:19). The challenge of the day for us is to look for another opportunity to travel with God. Just as Jesus spent each day looking for where the Father was working, so too the redeemed will join in with the Father, and they will walk through the day together. The days to come will be opportunities for the redeemed to further develop their intimate oneness with God. The redeemed should follow the pattern laid out by Jesus. The goal of Jesus was to follow the Father's lead, to accomplish God's plan for that particular day. It should be the same for the redeemed. As John writes, "And this is the way to have eternal life—to know you, the only true God, and Jesus Christ, the one you sent to earth" (John 17:3). Life will be an intimate exploration to know God in an inner experiential way.

Second, the land of the redeemed will be a land of truth. It will be a land where truth shapes every moment of the day. Dishonesty, even in the smallest degree, will be missing.

> '[T]he time is coming and is already here when true worshipers [worshippers] will worship the Father in spirit and in truth. The Father is looking for anyone who will worship him that way. For God is Spirit, so those who worship him must worship in spirit and in truth.' (John 4:23–24)

Had the Samaritan woman failed to be truthful with Jesus, she could have lost everything. But she responded with truth, and she gained everything. Deceit will have no place with God; it will have been banished. Lying tongues will have ceased to exist. False witnesses will be no more. Slanderous statements will never be heard again. The continually developing spiritual intimacy between God and every believer will have no sinister obstacles. Consistency of truth will be the standard. As Jesus said: "You are truly my disciples if you keep obeying my teachings. And you will know the truth, and the truth will set you free" (John 8:31–32). True freedom is only found in truth. Truth will banish all division and strife; the unity of truth will have a stabilizing effect. The redeemed will stand in the light of God's truth. There will be no vestige of fallenness. The redeemed will be pure and holy even as God is holy (1 Peter 1:16). The blood of Christ will have completed its task; his divine work within us will be perfect, rendering the believer free to grow in God. The corruption of sin will not torment the heart. The struggle with sin will be forever in the past. Truth will be the belt that encircles the redeemed (Ephesians 6:14).

Third, there won't be one ounce of prejudice among the redeemed. Nothing will spoil divine perfection. To know God experientially, to stand in the thoughts of God, to be clothed in the righteousness of God will forever silence wrong thinking. The redeemed will live in him (John 14:20). The seeds of division will not exist. There will be no fertile ground to foster any separation or isolation. The blemish of division will be unknown. The Samaritan woman found Jesus to be free from Jewish prejudices (John 4:9), and we will be like him. Everyone will be in a right standing with each other and with God. Genuine fidelity will be the standard. Accomplishing the will of God will know no barriers. Christlikeness will be an all-encompassing unifying principle. There will be no private hidden agendas stirring up strife. God's peace will flow uninterrupted.

Fourth, to know God is to have the ear of God, and God is always "ready to hear those who worship him and do his will" (John 9:31). Jesus was always confident that the Father heard him (John 11:42). This is the same confidence the redeemed will have throughout eternity. God readily seeks out and converses with those who are obedient (John 9:35–38). The formerly blind man may have been rejected by the Jewish leadership, but not by God. The formerly blind man had been loyal to the truth regardless of the personal cost to himself (John 9:30–33), and, in return, Jesus demonstrated his loyalty to the formerly blind man (John 9:35–39). The man had been thrown out of the synagogue (John 9:34), but Jesus openly searched for him, spoke to him, and encouraged him even though the disapproving Pharisees were standing nearby (John 9:40).

Fifth, those who intimately know God hear his softly whispered commands, and then they obey. They do not fear their Lord—they are one with him. They are not troubled by a rebellious spirit that produces a state of separation from God.

Instead, a deep and lasting friendship exists between them. Jesus says, "I have loved you even as the Father has loved me. Remain in my love. When you obey me, you remain in my love, just as I obey my Father and remain in his love" (John 15:9–10). Unity of heart is a sign of intimacy. God demonstrated his love. He came down from heaven and took upon himself the likeness of man. He died that we might live forever. He gave up eternity so that we might inherit eternity. Where is the danger in that kind of love? What prompts so many to neglect this great love? Love and obedience are not in opposition to each other; they actually walk hand in hand. If one surrenders to love, there is no defeat, there is no shame; there is only the sweet embrace of God.

> 'I command you to love each other in the same way that I love you. And here is how to measure it—the greatest love is shown when people lay down their lives for their friends. You are my friends if you obey me. I no longer call you servants, because a master doesn't confide in his servants. Now you are my friends, since I have told you everything the Father told me.' (John 15:12–15)

Sixth, the land of the redeemed will be the home of those who live far above the norm. The physical restraints encountered in this life will not hold true in the future. The redeemed will be like their risen Savior. Jesus modeled what our likeness will be like in his post crucifixion appearances and during his earthly ministry. In bodily form, Jesus could defy normal physical limitations such as turning water into wine (John 2:6–10). In like manner, his knowledge was not limited to personal experiences. He told the Samaritan woman all about her life even though he had never been a part it (John 4:17–18). He could walk on water (John 6:19).

Jesus was remarkable, and the redeemed will be like him. The redeemed will have a physical body that can be touched and one that can touch others, but it will be glorified in a likeness similar to Jesus (1 John 3:2). Our bodies will be endued with supernatural power, enabling them to stand in the holy presence of God. The redeemed will face God and his supersized divine realm of wonder and awe. God will be there, the Son will be there, and the Holy Spirit will be there; they will be the greatest treasure of all. The redeemed will have the pleasure, the freedom, and the honor of getting equated with God—to know the One who created all life, the One who is life.

> In Heaven, the barriers between redeemed human beings and God will forever be gone. To look into God's eyes will be to see what we've always longed to see: the person who made us for his own good pleasure. (Alcorn, 2004, p. 175)

Seventh, the land of the redeemed will be marked with a sense of knowing. Do you recall the transfiguration where Jesus appeared with Moses and Elijah? Moses and Elijah lived hundreds of years before the disciples were ever born. Yet, the disciples immediately recognized both men in a single glance (Matthew 17:2–4). Everything will be changed, glorified, beautifully refashioned, but recognizable and fully known.

The power of God will shine through everything, making everything new, yet totally known. The redeemed will stand in his presence, in his new world, in his knowledge, in his thoughts, and in his love. God will set up his dwelling place upon the face of the earth (Revelation 21:1–7). God's glorious creation will no longer bear the marks of sin. Everything will be better than in the beginning because the new earth and the new heaven will have an additional resident. The creation of God will be known and experienced with God. All that Satan accomplished will be wiped clean from the earth (Revelation 21:4). All traces of his evil will have been purged; this will include all who stood with him in rebellion. There will be no agnostics, no atheists, no humanists, no liars, or unbelievers of any kind. The land of the redeemed will be fit for a King and his people, and the peace of God will rein forever more.

The Spirit's Call

There is one last thing that must be addressed: Humanity intuitively knows that there is a God. That reality is recorded in Romans: "For the truth about God is known to them instinctively. God has put this knowledge in their hearts" (1:19). According to that Scripture, there is a God-awareness residing within every man and woman. It is a universal awareness that reaches beyond the grave. It calls to them at night when they lay their heads down. It never ceases to whisper within the heart about a possible life after death. But not all will benefit from this God-implanted, intuitive knowledge of Him. So few ever stop and ponder the possible origins of this soft voice. Where might it come from? Surely, someone had to have placed it there. So few realize that it is God's divine invitation to embrace him; it is his upward call of a better life. It is his whisper that there is more.

This universal awareness did not give birth to itself. It is God himself tugging at the heartstrings of every man and woman. Why do so few search for the origin of this omnipresent call? The questions that need to be answered are: "Where does an omnipresent call come from? Why does the call seem to originate deep within the soul? How did it come to be there? Who could have placed it there? Why does the call have such an eternal sound? And if one is to be honest, nothing on earth seems to be keeping it alive, yet it persists. Why? Who is calling your name?"

This universal, pervasive call cannot be seen with the eye. It cannot be heard with the natural ear, yet it speaks deep within the soul of each person. Its origin is not flesh and blood. It is Spirit! Therefore, the secular world's attempt to ignore it or reduce it down to an evolutionary drive for survival is futile. An evolutionary drive for survival would only push one to focus on the here and now. Survival is a "now" concept—not a future concept. What good is the future if one does not survive the now?

This persistent call beckons each person to look up, to hope beyond the grave. In contrast, evolution should beckon one to focus on the here and now, the immediate. The wisdom of this world could never have correctly ascertained an awareness of God or the origin of his call because it is too busy rejecting the supernatural. This awareness of something more is not earthbound, it's not natural, and it's not from below.

This awareness, this call, originates from the One who created everything in the beginning. God is the source, but the world does not want God. God is calling us back into the Garden of Eden, and humankind needs to remember that "Eden's greatest attraction was God's presence" (Alcorn, 2004, p. 179). And that, unfortunately, creates a major problem. How will the world answer the Holy Spirit if the world has already rejected God? The Spirit's call will go unanswered, and, in so doing, hope will die. God sent his Son to restore hope. Jesus was and is the physical representation of God's trumpet call to life. Jesus is the entrance into the Kingdom of Heaven. A beautiful afterlife is based upon the Son of God.

The Book of Revelation outlines what is to come. The future accommodations in the land of the redeemed are divinely supernatural. The glory of what is to come originates in God. The proud and the arrogant will not reside in God's house. All who cloth themselves in lies, in falsehood, in dishonesty, and in idolatry will not enter. They are not properly dressed, and they will be thrown out (Matthew 22:11–13). Their ugliness will cease. It will not enter. The corrupt choose not to walk in the likeness of Jesus. Is it then any wonder that they end up in a completely different place? We are all traveling toward our final destination whether or not we want to admit it.

The Resurrection of Life

So if we continue to live in him, we won't sin either. But those who keep on sinning have never known him or understood who he is. Dear children, don't let anyone deceive you about this: When people do what is right, it is because they are righteous, even as Christ is righteous. But when people keep on sinning, it shows they belong to the Devil, who has been sinning since the beginning. But the son of God came to destroy these works of the devil. Those who have been born into God's family do not sin, because God's life is in them. So they can't keep on sinning, because they have been born of God. So now we can tell who are children of God and who are children of the Devil. Anyone who does not obey God's commands and does not love other Christians does not belong to God. (1 John 3:6–10)

The redeemed are clearly traveling further and further away from that which is perishing. Their destination is an imperishable land where death has been exchanged for life and mortality has been exchanged for immortality. The resurrection of the redeemed was purchased by the blood of Jesus Christ. He laid down his life that we might live through him. The concept of loss is such an integral part of this life that it seems unlikely that loss will become extinct one day, and a new day will dawn bringing with it a new earth and a new heaven. Nevertheless, when the redeemed die, loss will enter the grave with them one last time. When they rise at the resurrection, death and all concepts of loss will remain in the grave—entombed forever.

Through Christ, the redeemed will have an extraordinary life. The redeemed "will reign with him [Jesus Christ]" (2 Timothy 4:8). The redeemed will have become God's Kingdom, they will have become God's priest, and they will reign through him who was worthy (Revelation 5:9–10). "And they shall reign forever and ever" (Revelation 22:5). The land of the redeemed will be a rich land; it will be "a land flowing with milk and honey" (Exodus 3:8). The redeemed are currently learning and acquiring the skills they will utilize throughout eternity. The only question that remains is: "Will you be there?"

CHAPTER 7

I Am the Salvation of God

JESUS SPOKE THE TRUTH when he stated that he was the salvation of God; there is no other provision. There never was, nor will there ever be. "I am the way, the truth, and the life. No one can come to the Father except through me" (John 14:6).

> We must either embrace Jesus' claim that He is God's Son or reject it. There is no intellectually honest alternative, given Jesus' claim that He is the only solution to bridge the gap between our sinfulness and God's holiness: "I am the way, and the truth, and the life; *no one comes to the Father but though Me*" (John 14:6). (Jeffress, 2017, ps. 200–201)

Have you not heard that it was God who created the world (Genesis 1:1)? It was God who spoke everything into existence. It was God who established the boundaries (Proverbs 8:29). It was God who brought forth the grass and the trees (Genesis 1:11–12), and it was God who formed humankind (Genesis 2:7).

It was God who sent his Son into the world not to condemn the world, "but to save it" (John 3:17). Therefore, if an "unbeliever embraces the truth about God that creation reveals, God will make sure he or she receives the information about Jesus Christ necessary for salvation" (Jeffress, 2017, p. 206).

Of course, this means that all other gods and their respective religions are quite literally dead-ends. There is no life in them. Not one of them has the power to lead its travelers into eternal life. It was Jesus, the Son of God, who descended from heaven to show the way (John 3:13), and there is no ambiguity with his words. There is no salvation outside of him. Only he had the endorsement of God: "And a voice from heaven said, 'This is my beloved Son, and I am fully pleased with him'" (Matthew 3:17). The Bible is true in singling out Jesus and the work he accomplished. Believers in Christ could count on him, and the Scriptures declared: "The godly will inherit the land and will live there forever" (Psalm 37:29), but the wicked have no future (Psalm 37:38). Jesus was who he claimed to be, the Son of God, the one who had descended to save humanity.

> It is perfectly clear then that this is the testimony that Jesus wanted to bear of Himself. We also see that the Jews must have understood His reply as a claim to His being God. There were two alternatives to be faced then; that His assertions were pure blasphemy or that He was God. (McDowell, 1999, p. 140)

Search throughout the history of humankind, and you will find that Jesus was unique. As was stated earlier, the Bible has the greatest historical documentation of any book from antiquity. Whether the world likes it or not, Jesus is a part of human history. Biblical and nonbiblical sources are available that historically verify his walk with humanity. For instances, Hugo Grotius, a historical writer and an expert in international law, wrote extensively about Christianity. He was born in 1583,

I Am the Salvation of God

and he died in 1645. He felt that the evidence for Christ was overwhelming.

> Grotius begins by pointing out that it is certain that Jesus of Nazareth was an actual historical person living in Judea under the reign of Tiberius. This fact is acknowledged in historical writings from Christians, Jews, and pagans alike. Further, he was put to death and thereafter worshiped by men. The reason for this worship was that he had performed various miracles during his life. Many of the early Christians such as Polycarp, Irenaeus, Athenagoras, Origen, Tertullian, Clement of Alexandria, and so forth were raised in other religions, yet came to worship this man Jesus as God, because they had made a diligent inquiry and discovered that he had wrought many miraculous deeds. (Craig, 2008, p. 213)

Jesus, a historical figure, was the Son of Man (Matthew 18:11) and he was also the Son of God (John 3:16). Jesus was the common ground between humanity and God. He inherited humanity from his mother, Mary, and Jesus inherited divinity from his heavenly Father (Luke 1:35). He was not born under sin like all the other descendants of Adam. He was born without a sin nature. This fact is what set Jesus apart. He was the blending of untainted humanity and divinity into one person.

As you well know, the blood of the mother does not come into contact with the fetus, and neither did Mary's blood come into contact with Jesus. Therefore, he was not touched by Mary's sin-tainted blood. All Jesus inherited from Mary was the likeness of mankind. This inheritance from his mother gave him the right to represent humanity before God. He became one with humankind, sharing in our likeness. Based upon his human birthright, Jesus could participate in the history of the world. And, in so doing, he could take on the sin debt of humanity, and that was the reason for Jesus' birth.

I Am the Christ

Jesus had the power to make permanent changes upon mankind's eternity based upon his eternal nature. Jesus once stated, "You are from below; I am from above. You are of this world; I am not'" (John 8:23). He was bringing life from above. He was sent into the world by his Father (John 3:17). Jesus existed long before the foundations of this world were ever set, and that he had the love of his Father upon him (John 17:24). The author Josh McDowell writes: "His claim was to a unique relationship with God as His Father. Just as a human father's son must be fully human, God's Son must be fully God. All that the Father is, the Son is" (1999, p. 142).

The Old Testament records the existence of a King David. This King David lived hundreds of years before Jesus was ever born, yet he referred to Jesus as his Lord (Matthew 22:41–45). That was because Jesus existed before King David was born. In fact, Jesus was present when Adam and Eve were created, and they were created in his image, and in the Father's image, and in the Holy Spirit's image (Genesis 1:26).

Jesus entered our world through a virgin (Matthew 1:18–25). Has any other man ever been born of a virgin? No! Has any other man ever been born by the power of the Holy Spirit (Matthew 1:18)? No! No man before Jesus or after Jesus ever possessed both humanity and divinity. Therefore, Jesus was the common ground between the temporal and the eternal. Jesus was the only one qualified to be the mediator between us and God. Jesus was the salvation of God. Jesus was the Christ; he was the Messiah. The Gospel record does not hesitate in making it known that Jesus was the Son of God. As Josh McDowell writes: "Jesus, in many cases, made known His deity indirectly by both His words and His actions" (1999, p. 148).

Equally important was his purpose for coming into the world. He came to pay a debt he did not owe; we were the ones who owed a debt we could not pay. Jesus became one with humanity so that he could legally take our debt upon himself. He came to lay down his life that others might live (John 10:11). Jesus once told Nicodemus that "unless you are born again, you can never see the Kingdom of God" (John 3:3). This was a true statement regardless if Nicodemus struggled with the concept. Struggling with a new concept is not an indicator that the concept is less than truthful.

We can know God without totally comprehending God. And, if God is God, we should anticipate that there will be much that we do not understand. Therefore, any lack of comprehension on our part does not diminish the Word of God. God's knowledge and thinking are far above ours (Isaiah 55:8–9), but not knowing everything about someone is not new to us.

In general, when we know someone, we never know them at 100 percent. There is a percentage in every relationship that falls into the unknown. We take the unknown part of the relationship by faith in light of all that we do know about a particular person. I know my wife, but I still do not know her 100 percent. Wouldn't this be true to a greater degree with God? I have been married for forty-seven years, and my wife still leaves me scratching my head. Faith seems to be an integral part of every interaction with others. We really do not have an excuse for applying a negative attitude about faith when it comes to God. I do not know everything about God, but I have learned that he is honest, reliable, and truthful. So, if he says something that I do not understand, I'm confident that I will come to an understanding at some point in the future. Does that seem far-fetched to you? Well, let me ask another question. When you and your wife come to a disagreement about something, is she ever wrong? I'm sorry? Did you say something? I didn't hear you? I didn't think so. Or, do you usually come around and say, *yes dear*? I rest my case. Shall we move on?

Returning to the concept of being born again, Jesus continues explaining it this way: "Humans can reproduce only human life, but the Holy Spirit gives new life from heaven" (John 3:6). Jesus was and still is that life! Those who believe in him, those who trust in him, those who turn to him will have eternal life (John 3:16). Jesus knew that Nicodemus did not understand everything he was saying, but that did not matter. Our limited understanding does not disqualify truth. Without God's intervention, eternity would be beyond human reach. Being born again is a spiritual concept, and Jesus was speaking about spiritual things, eternal things, that were beyond our complete understanding.

However, a complete understanding is not a pre-requisite to believing. A complete understanding is not a pre-requisite to obedience. Consider the roles of parents. They place demands upon their children that the children do not always understand or agree with, but that does not stop the parent. Parents simply state what will be, and children can either obey or face the consequences for their actions. Do we think that we are better parents than God?

In the Gospel of John, we read: "Those who don't obey the Son will never experience eternal life, but the wrath of God remains upon them" (3:36). You are not the first to struggle with the words of God, and you will not be the last. Nevertheless, his words are clear enough, and his warning stands firm. Jesus continued to speak the truth during his earthly ministry. Consider the following words: 'The highway to hell is broad, and its gate is wide for the many who choose the easy way. But the gateway to life is small, and the road is narrow, and only a few ever find it'" (Matthew 7:13–14).

The Gateway Is Small

Without a doubt, these words of Jesus should have made you pause. The gateway is small? Well, how small is small? Do you know? Those words carry an eternal warning, one that should not be ignored. Did the warning raise the hair on the back of your neck? It should have! Jesus further stated that only a few individuals ever find this narrow road. Why is that true? Have you ever paused long enough to wonder? Or, does Jesus' statement seem too far away at the present? If so, that is a common mistake. The rich man in Luke 12:16–20 made the same mistake. His goal was to build bigger barns to store everything he might need for years to come, but he did not have many years ahead of him. His life suddenly ended! The accountability that seemed so remote and so far away was upon him. Suddenly his time was up.

Don't make his mistake and count on what is not yours. He assumed that he had all the time in the world. After all, he was successful. He had plenty of wealth, and it seemed only natural that he would live for many more years, but he didn't. Many people do not live to a ripe old age and many fail to search for truth when they feel so full of life. Is it then any wonder that so few ever find truth? It is just too easy to allow life to slip by one moment at a time. So many foolishly think they have the luxury of waiting for just one more minute; they are too busy living to consider the prospect of dying. But, before they know it, an entire lifetime has slipped by.

Suddenly, the gate is closed and the opportunity for life is forfeited. The gateway to life is comparatively very small when you stop to notice all of the distracting things standing between you and that gate. It is like trying to spot one individual in the midst of millions of others. What an impossible task! One among millions is terribly small, but Jesus was that one out of a million. Better yet, he was actually more like one out of billions. That's why an entire book was written about him. That's why the book recorded his life, his ministry, and the many miracles he performed. God highlighted his life. In fact, God turned the light of the Scriptures upon his Son. Jesus was and still is the gate (John 10:9), and everyone who desires life must pass through him before it is too late.

Jesus tells us: "So don't worry about having enough food or drink or clothing . . . Your heavenly Father already knows all of your needs, and he will give you all you need from day to day

I Am the Christ

if you live for him and make the kingdom of God your primary concern" (Matthew 6:31–33). Are you starting to catch on? By simply making the Kingdom of God your primary concern, you shrink down all of the distracting obstacles in your path. With God as your center point, all of the distracting obstacles in this world lose their devastating impact upon your vision. The decisive issue is whether a person obeys God or not (Matthew 7:21). A person may appear religious, but that will not automatically make him or her right with God. God will not judge based upon outward appearances (John 7:24). He will look much deeper. He will search out the deepest portions of an individual's heart, mind, and soul. Everyone's motivations will be exposed in the end. Nothing will remain hidden from his sight; everything will be brought into the light (Luke 12:2–3).

The gateway is no wider than Jesus' shoulders. Everyone must turn and face him before they can enter into his Father's kingdom. Everyone who enters will have had to acknowledge Jesus as God's provision or there will be no entry. No one can do this for you; you must enter on your own volition. You must come to terms with Jesus! Your entry will be personal, or it will not be at all. You must come as you are; you must come while you can. Jesus was and still is the gateway to life, and the dead shall not be allowed to pass through. Those are God's conditions, and he will not change his mind (Malachi 3:6, Hebrews 13:8, James 1:17). You may enter through Jesus, or you will die in your sins (Luke 13:3), and forever be lost.

"The highway to hell is broad, and its gate is wide for the many who choose the easy way. But the gateway to life is small, and the road is narrow, and only a few ever find it" (Matthew 7:13–14). In the preceding verse, the road to life is depicted as being narrow. How narrow is this narrow road? Have you ever taken the time to ponder this concept?

I Am the Salvation of God

The Road Is Narrow

There are many things in life that are beyond our ability to control or to change, and the narrowness of the road happens to be one of those things. We cannot make the road any wider. We cannot dictate its course or direction, but we can choose to ignore it. We can even pretend that is does not exist, but in the end that will prove to be catastrophic. So, does it matter how narrow the road may be? Yes!

The road to life is no wider than the beam Jesus was crucified upon. It was paved with his blood. It was covered with his pain and agony. Woe to those who spurn his sacrifice. Woe to those who marginalize his death.

The heavenly Father went to great lengths to redeem humankind. He demonstrated his unconditional love for us. For it was God, the Father, who withheld his mighty hand as Jesus was mocked; he did not defend his Son. God stood silent when we scourged his Son to within an inch of his life. And there must have been tears streaming down God's face as we crucified his Son. The screams of God's Son went unanswered as the nails were driven into his flesh. God endured all this that we might live. His love for us knew no limits.

In light of this great cost, what do you think God's reaction will be toward those who reject his gift of love? Do you think he will sit idly by and pout? Think for just a moment. If your brother laid down his life to save someone, and that person spurned the sacrifice, what would you say to that ungrateful person? What would be your response? I would be willing to wager that your response would not be mild or passive. Nor would it be pleasant; it would be a sudden cataclysmic event. Your response would be equal to the value of the gift rejected.

We must remember that Jesus' gift was eternal! The eternal Son of God stepped down out of eternity into our temporal world to lay down his life for us. Jesus was the gift. The gift came down from heaven. It was an offer of eternal love. His sacrifice was offered in loving kindness. He was cruelly beaten. He was mocked. He was crucified, and none of it was pleasant. If anyone is foolish enough to reject his eternal gift, they will be greeted with eternal consequences. All who dismiss Jesus' sacrifice will be met with an eternal state of misery, heartbreak, and sorrow. Jesus' death upon the cross "is the power of God at work, saving everyone who believes" (Romans 1:16).

> For if you confess with your mouth that Jesus is Lord and believe in your heart that God raised him from the dead, you will be saved. For it is by believing in your heart that you are made right with God, and it is by confessing with your mouth that you are saved. (Romans 10:9–10)

Unquestionably, the road to life is narrow, but it is not impossible to navigate. Everyone simply needs to follow the Scriptures and the leading of the Holy Spirit (John 14:26). The Scriptures are your blueprint for life—not death. The Scriptures do not take away from life; they add life. They are life. The Scriptures speak of being transformed into Jesus' image (2 Corinthians 3:18), and the more you are transformed into his image, the freer you become. The cross brought freedom from the bondage of sin and death. He who has been set free is free indeed (John 8:36).

The world would have you think that the Bible restricts life when the opposite is actually true. "Those who obey my commandments are the ones who love me. And because they love me, my Father will love them and I will love them. And I will reveal myself to each one of them" (John 14:21). To know God and to be known by God is not the hallmark of a repressed life. It is the beginning of life. The world has conditioned itself into thinking that obedience disrupts self-actualization. How sad! How terribly destructive! Each person who falls into this deadly trap of self-exaltation will only find death, and each person who makes this fatal mistake adds to the congestion of the road most traveled.

Jesus said: "The highway to hell is broad, and its gate is wide for the many who choose the easy way" (Matthew 7:13). Why do you think the highway to hell is so broad, and the gate is so wide? Because the highway and the gate must be broad to accommodate the thousands upon thousands of travelers who have chosen to march shoulder to shoulder toward their own destruction. The highway to hell is the easier road to travel because it runs downhill. On the other hand, the road less traveled leads toward life, heading upward—always upward. It is so sad that going with the flow always seems easier.

So, if there are two roads, how does one know which road he or she has chosen to travel? Let's start with the word *obedience*. How does the word *obedience* fit into your mouth? Does it sound repulsive? Does it have a distasteful flavor? Where does God fit into your life? Where does the Son of God fit? Do you rely upon his work? Do you even know what he did on your behalf? Can you call him Lord? Do you bow your knee before him? Do you honor him with your life? Does he fill your thoughts? Is your life heavily influenced by his Father's commandments? Or, do all of these questions seem alien and completely out of place to you?

Let's try this approach. Are you traveling in the opposite direction from the masses? Do you stick out and appear to be out of step with the world? I sincerely hope you do. Jesus never really fit in either. The world outright rejected him. In fact, it actually wanted him dead, but they would not be allowed to kill him until the appointed time (John 7:30).

How are you faring in a world hostile toward Jesus Christ? Do you fit in? Are you encountering worldly rejection? Or, does your life mirror the world's agenda? Is your life producing fruit that looks just like theirs? In Matthew we read: "A tree is identified by its fruit. Make a tree good, and its fruit will be good" (Matthew 12:33). Well? What do you see? When you turn around and look at your life's fruit, what do you see? Is it a crop of self? Have you sown and harvested a crop of self-glorification? Are you the meaning of your life? Does your career provide all the meaning you need? Are you the summation of all there is about you? If you are, you are not alone; the masses are traveling down that same broad highway. Living in the presence of God is not popular, but it does hold the promise of life.

Let's turn the words of Jesus back onto him. Let's look at the fruit he produced. We should not exempt him from his own words. What kind of fruit did he produce? The Gospels record his manner of life with the following: Jesus regularly taught on the Sabbath in the synagogues, leaving the people in amazement (Mark 1:21–22). He silenced and cast out demons (Mark 1:24–25). Jesus healed many who were sick (Mark 1:29–34). He healed a man with leprosy (Mark 1:41). He preached and ministered to the masses (Mark 2:1–2). Jesus healed a paralyzed man (Mark 2:5). He openly demonstrated his authority, allowing his adversaries to observe his actions (Mark 2:8–12). Jesus demonstrated patience toward his adversaries (Mark 2:15–17). He demonstrated a willingness to answer questions (Mark 2:18–22). Jesus was willing to answer questions even when confronted with hostility (Mark 2: 23–28). His life's fruit openly established his kindness, his generosity, his power, and his divinity. He was a righteous man. His fruit openly proves that he was not a fraud. "Someone who lived as Jesus lived, taught as Jesus taught, and died as Jesus died could not have been a liar" (McDowell, 1999, p. 160).

Not surprisingly, obedience becomes a major component of the narrow road where God enlightens the mind. It is a road where each step brings you closer to God and further away from the world. The true reality of life and the truthfulness of

I Am the Salvation of God

the Scriptures begin to come more and more into focus. This process occurs because the maturing believer begins to think the thoughts of God to a greater and greater degree, and their life changes as a result. Miraculously, the Scriptures and life merge into a strange oneness never seen before, and life lived in the shadow of the Scriptures takes on a much deeper meaning. The purpose for life is found; it is hidden in the midst of obedience. As the eyes of understanding open and one's destiny begins to become obvious. The Bible is no longer a boring list of dos and don'ts, but a road map for life. The life spoken of within the Word of God takes on a whole new meaning. The many former distractions of life begin to fade, becoming smaller and smaller, and the narrow road becomes a more familiar sight. *Obedience is no longer a curse word associated with chains and drudgery.*

The psalmist writes: "Taste and see that the Lord is good" (Psalm 34:8). How many of you can glance at a meal from a great distance and know how it will taste? If you are being honest, no one can. One must sit down and dig in before the quality, the flavor, and the richness of the meal can be experienced. Yet, many try from a great distance to evaluate God, and it leaves them full of loathing and despair. But this is the wrong approach. Following the words of the psalmist requires action. "Taste and see that the Lord is good. Oh, the joys of those who trust in him!" (Psalm 34:8). How else can you learn and experience what God has prepared for you if you fail to act? Stop rejecting his offer of life from afar. "Only fools say in their heart, 'There is no God'" (Psalm 14:1). In spite of the world's rejection of God, the followers of God have tasted, and they know the richness of God.

> The law of the Lord is perfect reviving the soul. The decrees of the Lord are trustworthy, making wise the simple. The commandments of the Lord are right, bringing joy to the heart. The commands of the Lord are clear, giving insight to life. Reverence for the Lord is pure, lasting

forever. The laws of the Lord are true, each one is fair. They are more desirable than gold, even the finest gold. They are sweeter than honey, even honey dripping form the comb. They are a warning to those who hear them; there is great reward for those who obey them. (Psalm 19:7–11)

Everyone who has decided to follow the Lord undergoes a transforming process where their true identity begins to emerge. The chains of the world break, hindrances weaken, and their God-given worth and purpose becomes apparent. Humanity was never designed to walk through life separated and out of step with God. Humanity was simply not created in an alienated state in the beginning (Genesis 3:8); Adam could fellowship with God, and now, once again, through Jesus' death we can walk with God. In Psalm 37:23–24, we read: "The steps of the godly are directed by the Lord. He delights in every detail of their lives. Though they stumble, they will not fall, for the Lord holds them by the hand."

The gateway is small and the road is narrow, but those who travel along this path experience a spiritual shift. For some, the change will be a massive character change. For others it may be a change in their language or a change in attitude. For others it may be a change in how they relate to those around them. No matter how the changes may appear, the changes will reveal the presence of God. This newness of character and this newness of life will reflect the image of Jesus. He commanded all that would follow him "to love each other in the same way that I have loved the Father" (John 15:12).

The Bible provides the necessary daily guidance you need, but you must read it and ponder its meaning. Search for the life offered. In addition to your own efforts, the Holy Spirit will be with you providing individual tutoring services. Remember, Jesus said: "I will ask the Father, and he will give you another

I Am the Salvation of God

Counselor, who will never leave you. He is the Holy Spirit, who leads into all truth" (John 14:16–17). Look for the divine road signs along the way; obey the signs you encounter, and you will remain on the narrow road. Remember, you will not be traveling alone. The Spirit of God will be your traveling companion every step of the way (John 16:13).

To be sure, the world will not understand you, and the world will begin to hate you because it will sense that you are no longer a part of it (John 15:18–21). Unfortunately, this will be one of the changes you will encounter. Jesus said: "When the world hates you, remember it hated me before it hated you. The world would love you if you belonged to it, but you don't" (John 15:18). The world is at odds with God, and now that you are a part of the family of God it will be at odds with you. To be saved is to be translated out of this dying kingdom and into God's kingdom. You are now citizens of heaven; you are children of God, and you will know the love of God. Jesus also said: "Remain in my love. When you obey me, you remain in my love, just as I obey my Father and remain in his love" (John 15:9). There it is again! The concept of *obedience*! What are we to do with this word? This word gets caught in the throat of the dying, but it really shouldn't cause the believer to choke.

In fact, everyone obeys something. No one is exempt. Obedience to something is the outward expression of an inward condition. If one is inwardly connected to God, then that individual should live a life which denotes the presence of God. In other words, conforming to God and listening to God are essential characteristics of a spiritual walk with God. You are not to grieve over your dying connection to the world. The world is heading straight toward a collision course with the coming wrath of God. As a believer, you are not! A believer should be honoring God with their life and learning to walk with God; they should be following Jesus' example. Honor the commandments of God; learn through experience the inner meaning and hidden treasure of God's commandments. The apostle Paul wrote about this very thing in his letter to the believers in Rome.

> And so, dear brothers and sisters, I plead with you to give your bodies to God. Let them be a living and holy sacrifice—the kind he will accept. When you think of what he has done for you, is this too much to ask? Don't copy the behavior and customs of this world. But let God transform you into a new person by changing the way you think. Then you will know what God wants you to do, and you will know how good and pleasing and perfect his will really is. (Romans 12:1–2)

Obedience is not a word to be dreaded. Let me say it again: everybody obeys something or someone. Those who are of this world conform, follow, or obey the world because they are a part of it. They belong to the world; they comply or obey it because it is what they are. It is just the natural order of things. This is why Paul wrote: "Don't copy the behavior and customs of this world." If someone copies or conforms to this dying world, they do so because they are of the world, but for those who believe in Jesus there is a new way to live. God has provided road signs—commandments—for the believer's benefit. The road signs are vital for spiritual progress. Do not shrink from words like *commandments* or *obedience*. If you do, you need to realize that the repulsion comes from your old sinful nature. It does not want its connection to the world severed, but you must remember that something must die. Either a person's sin nature must suffer loss or the person's soul must suffer loss. Both cannot thrive at the same time. One needs more of the world while the other needs more of the Spirit.

Jesus said: "The world's sin is unbelief in me" (John 16:9). Because the world does not believe in Jesus' sacrifice, there is no provision for them. Therefore, they will quite literally die in their sin (John 8:24). For the ones who believe in Christ and in his resurrection, there is eternal life. His blood has the power to create a new creature, and that new creature can and will enter into the presence of God. Eternity has already begun for the believer, but for the unbeliever there is only death. Just as Judas chose to go "'out into the night'" (John 13:30), so too will many choose to follow the same destructive path. So, the road to destruction must be broad to accommodate all those who obediently follow the world's system.

Peace with God Is Possible

If you haven't figured it out yet, it should start becoming more and more obvious with every passing moment. Obedience is not the real issue at hand. The real issue is hidden deep within each person. A person's obedience is an expression or a by-product of the heart. Obedience flows from what is lurking within each individual. Your outward, daily expressions are the by-product of the inward condition of the heart. In other words, your life reveals what is not obvious to the naked eye. For example, Jesus loved his Father, and that love compelled him to be obedient to the Father's plan. His obedience to the Father meant that he would bring salvation to humanity no matter the cost. In fact, it was accomplished in spite of the shame, the humiliation, and the pain. It was God's plan from the beginning that Jesus would come into our world and lay down his life that we might live.

Spiritual freedom for humanity had to be purchased. It came at a terrible price, but it was a free gift to us. Consider World War I and World War II. How many lives had to be sacrificed for the cause of freedom? The cost was born by those who died— those who poured out their blood. They paid a terrible price so their children and their children's children could live free. Nevertheless, the freedom they purchased was only temporary, but the freedom Jesus purchased was, and still is, eternal. In obedience, Jesus was born into a world he had created. He humbled himself, taking on the form of a man. He purchased eternal peace between God and humankind. He provided what no other man could ever purchase. No one else could or would come from above to pay the price he paid. Therefore, there is simply no salvation outside of Jesus Christ. His obedience, his sacrifice would never be seen again. Woe to those who chose to neglect this "great salvation that was announced by the Lord Jesus himself" (Hebrews 2:3).

Undeniably, the announcement did not come naked, barren, or empty, but the announcement came with spiritual certifications from heaven. The writer of Hebrews points out that "God verified the message by signs and wonders and various miracles" (2:4). These powerful signs were all provided for us—that we might know, beyond any shadow of a doubt, the truthfulness of the announcement. The salvation Jesus offered was authentic; it was the real deal. It procured the forgiveness people needed, and the justice God demanded. However, salvation is not activated until a person calls upon the name of Jesus, trusting and accepting in his sacrifice. Salvation comes strictly through his work. In fact, the Gospels record many events where heavenly certifications accompanied his actions. One such event is recorded below:

> Some people brought to him a paralyzed man on a mat. Seeing their faith, Jesus said to the paralyzed man, "Take heart, son! Your sins are forgiven." "Blasphemy! This man talks like he is God!" some of the teachers of religious law said among themselves. Jesus knew what they were thinking, so he asked them, "Why are you thinking such evil thoughts? Is it easier to say, 'Your sins are forgiven' or 'Get up and walk'? I will prove that I, the Son of Man, have the authority on earth to forgive sins." Then Jesus turned to the paralyzed man and said, "Stand up, take your mat, and go on home, because you are healed!" And the man jumped up and went home! Fear swept through the crowd as they saw this happen right before their eyes.

They praised God for sending a man with such great authority. (Matthew 9:2–8)

Despite the evidence, some, like the religious leaders above, refuse to see the truth. But once again, truth is not dependent upon anyone's approval. The Scriptures accurately portray Jesus' earthly ministry, and his many post-resurrection appearances (Act 1:3). If people truly want to know the truth, the truth is available.

The problem is not a lack of evidence. It is a heart problem! There is ample evidence to convict the unbelievers of the coming judgment of Almighty God. The unbelievers will stand condemned, and they will be sentenced to an eternal damnation. If that happens, it will be the product of their stubborn hearts. Jesus did his part! He was born. He lived as a man. He loved without limits or prejudice. He spoke the truth. Jesus warned everyone willing to listen, and he laid down his life. Jesus' words are documented throughout the Gospels. And according to Charles Leslie, a theological and political writer in the late seventeenth to early eighteenth century, the reliability and the accuracy of the Scriptures has been firmly established.

> He [Charles Leslie] argues that when one examines the biblical narratives as one would any matter of fact, one will find them to be historically reliable. Hence, he maintains that one must either reject all the historical works of classical antiquity or else admit the Gospel accounts along with them. (Craig, 2008, p. 215)

Based on the evidence, the words of Jesus and his resurrection are historical facts. When Jesus rose from the dead, everyone who would believe in him rose with him (1 Corinthians 6:14). And, based upon the historical documents that attest to the truthfulness of the Bible, every Christian has been translated into the kingdom of God (Colossians 1:13). Therefore, to reject the

Gospel accounts is to reject all historical works. This would be an unjustifiable course of action, and an eternal state of anguish awaits everyone who takes this route. The stubborn of heart will be "cast out" as described in the Gospels.

Jesus personally warned the religious leaders with his words, and with his actions (Matthew 9:4–8). He did not reject them for their evil thinking. In fact, he exposed their private judgmental words with a tailored warning (Mathew 9:4–8), and the Holy Spirit's convicting power was surely present. Jesus confronted their evil with patience and kindness by demonstrating his knowledge of their evil thoughts. His persistent willingness to provide them with opportunities to repent without repercussions was repeated over and over. Then, Jesus followed up his words with proof that was tangible. He publicly healed the paralyzed man. It was Jesus' gift to the religious leaders. The Father certified the Son's words and actions with divine power and patience.

God laid it all out for their inspection. God actually submitted himself to the scrutiny of the religious leadership, and the Son of God submitted himself as well. His love freely fell on everyone. In his eyes, the religious leaders were far more crippled than the paralyzed man because their infirmities were deep-seated and self-inflicted. The religious leaders were cloaked in and chocking in their own self-righteousness. Their sin had the stink of death. Yet, Jesus truly wanted everyone, including the religious leaders, to rise up and freely walk into his loving forgiveness. But the religious leaders were not willing to see the spiritual proofs being provided. They refused their badly needed healing from their self-righteousness. The religious leaders were not the superior ones in this encounter. They needed Jesus' approval; Jesus did not need theirs.

Let's compare the historical record of antiquity. How much proof is actually out there in support of the Bible? Does the historical record single out the Bible as some unusual book? Yes! First, there are thousands of proofs out there for our inspection:

I Am the Salvation of God

"[W]e have close to, if not more than, 25,000 manuscript copies of portions of the New Testament in existence today" (McDowell, 1999, p. 34). Let's remember that history has its own voice. Our job is to listen. If we search, we will find that Jesus is a part of the world's history. He was with God the Father and God the Holy Spirit long before any of us were ever born. He entered our world to save us, and our eternity hinges upon what he accomplished. And we had better know our history because God will hold us accountable.

Second, there are more copies and partial copies of the books of the Bible than any other book from antiquity. "No other document of antiquity even begins to approach such numbers and attestations" (McDowell, 1999, p. 34). Do you think the Bible preserved itself? Do you think it happened by chance? Do you really think God won't hold us responsible? He will! God's hand preserved the Bible so that we would be confident in the message it contains.

Third, the death and crucifixion of Jesus Christ represents the most-documented case of any man's death from the ancient world (McDowell, 1999, p. 212). This documentation establishes the fact that accuracy and reliability are important factors to God. He has made it historically possible for us to know that his Son laid down his life for us. Therefore, God will be totally justified when he demands an accounting from every person who has ever lived. Every life is subject to the actions of the Son of God. Without a doubt, Jesus has left his life-giving mark upon the face of the earth. And I suppose that is why Satan will one day, in the near future, want to leave his mark upon the face of the earth—the mark of the beast, 666 (Revelation 13:16–18).

Fourth, eyewitnesses to some of the events recorded in the Bible were still living when the accounts were first written. That means that any lies told to embellish Jesus' life or his ministry or his crucifixion and resurrection could have been refuted with ease. From these facts, it becomes abundantly clear that God is interested in accountability, and he has left us an accounting of his Son's actions. What do you think he will require of us?

> When an event takes place in history and there are enough people alive who were eyewitnesses of it or had participated in the event, and when the information is published, one is able to verify the validity of an historical event (circumstantial evidence). (McDowell, 1999, p. 215)

The apostle Paul's own writing occurred within twenty-five years of the resurrection of Jesus Christ (McDowell, 1999, p. 214). The historical work of Jesus Christ is a fact. No reasonable person can effectively ignore the historical record.

In addition, there are various authors of this present time who have dedicated their lives to studying the historical reliability of the Scriptures. Therefore, modern man will be held accountable. Truth has been made available. The historicity of the Bible has been adequately documented, and, if an individual has neglected or rejected, or has chosen to remain ignorant about the content of the Bible, that will not be a viable justification for not coming to a saving faith. History can be analyzed and studied in the same way a geologist can analyze and study in the field of geology.

> For the subject matter of the geologist is every bit as indirect as that of the historian, and yet geology is part of science, which has traditionally been the model of objectivity to the relativist. Since lack of direct access cannot preclude geological knowledge, neither can it preclude historical knowledge. (Craig, 2008, p. 227)

Therefore, choosing to remain blind will be counted as sin, and it will be judged as such (John 9:39–41). "God shows his anger from heaven against all sinful, wicked people who push the truth away from themselves. For the truth about God is known to them instinctively. God has put this knowledge in their hearts" (Romans 1:18–19).

Salvation is but a breath away, but so is eternal judgment. Some tend to put this decision to the side feeling that they have plenty of time, but they may not. Are they, or are you, the master of time? No! No one knows his or her final hour; death can come suddenly without any warning. When you put this decision off, you are gambling with your soul

> As surely as I live, says the Sovereign Lord, I take no pleasure in the death of wicked people. I only want them to turn from their wicked ways so they can live. Turn! Turn from your wickedness, O people of Israel! Why should you die? (Ezekiel 33:11)

Jesus came to Earth to lay down his life, knowing that death could not hold him down. "For I have the right to lay it down when I want to and also the power to take it again. For my Father has given me this command" (John 10:18). Everyone who trusts in Jesus shall live through him, and they "will live in the house of the Lord forever" (Psalm 23:6). But those who have not trusted in him still struggle with an unseen enemy, and that enemy is sin. It whispers deep within the recesses of their hearts, leaving them with no profound respect for God to restrain them (Psalm 36:1). Whereas, the godly "fill their hearts with God's law, so they will never slip from his path" (Psalm 37:31). Did you notice the words of wisdom quoted to you just now? Those who believe in God may still stumble, and they may fall many more times before their time is up, but they will not slip off the right path. They will not fall from God's grace; they will not depart from the narrow road.

There is an art to living well in this life, and the godly have found it. They do not walk alone. They do not rely upon a world that is beset with so many limitations. Their destination does not lie below, but far above. The world's wisdom cannot lead anyone

I Am the Christ

to a place beyond its comprehension: "For just as the heavens are higher than the earth, so are my ways higher than your ways and my thoughts higher than your thoughts" (Isaiah 11:9). You must follow Jesus' example. He stepped down off of his throne and surrendered to the will of the Father that we might live forever. He laid down eternity so that we might inherit eternity through his blood. How long will you hold out? Will you realize too late? Can you match his actions? Are you willing to step down off of your throne and surrender your life to him? Jesus can keep what you will only lose in the end, and he makes this point extremely clear: "If you try to keep your life for yourself, you will lose it. But if you give up your life for me, you will find true life" (Matthew 16:25).

By surrendering his life to the Father's plan, many have come to know true life. Jesus had this true life from the beginning; the Father, the Holy Spirit, and Son existed long before our world was ever created (Genesis 1:1–2, 1:26; Psalm 102:25; John 1:1–2; Colossians 1:15–17). To live in the presence of God is true life, but we must step down off of our throne. Can you meet him at the cross? Through his sacrifice, eternal life can be yours. There has never been a greater act of selflessness. There has never been a greater act of love. To love is to be willing to lay down everything (Philippians 2:6–8). His coming into our world, his suffering, his rejection, his death, and his resurrection were not mindless acts. It was a divine plan. There was reason and intent in his willingness to set aside everything and come to you. God doesn't expect you to fully understand. The angels of God are "eagerly watching" God's plan unfold (1 Peter 1:12). We were separated from God by our sin, but now, through Jesus' blood, we can be separated from our sin, becoming a new creation (2 Corinthians 5:17). God wanted you to know his world—a place of unlimited love, a place of unconditional acceptance, a place of fellowship and eternal forgiveness.

I Am the Salvation of God

Without any reservation or hesitation, God is now asking you to surrender to him and to stand in the love of the Son of God just as Jesus stood in the Father's love.

> "Don't you believe that I am in the Father and the Father is in me? The words I say are not my own, but my Father who lives in me does his work through me. Just believe that I am in the Father and the Father is in me. Or at least believe because of what you have seen me do." (John 14:10–14)

Jesus said: "Those who obey my commandments are the ones who love me. And because they love me, my Father will love them, and I will love them. And I will reveal myself to each one of them" (John 14:21). No one needs to hesitate. Jesus' love is real. He came and died that we might join with him—for all eternity. Jesus laid down his life, showing his willingness to be our friend. Jesus wants you to join with him and him with you. Yet, he will not force his love upon you. You may remain in a dying world and perish with it, or you may leave death behind and live in his love. His love is patient and kind, and it will last forever (1 Corinthians 13:4–8).

Jesus will not turn anyone away when he or she comes in spirit and in truth. This was proven through his encounter with the Samaritan woman at the well (John 4:23–24). He didn't care what her life had been. He only wanted to know what she would be—both in that moment and in the future. Obviously, the opposite is equally true. A person who willfully closes their eyes and remains untruthful cannot truly surrender to Jesus. They cannot stand in his love. Their very thoughts and actions are a rejection of his love. No one can reject the supernatural and claim to love God who is Spirit. Can anyone surrender to Jesus while rejecting his supernatural birth, his divine identity, his purpose for coming, or his joining of humanity and divinity? Jesus is Spirit and he is Truth.

The love of Jesus and the love of the Father can only be accessed by faith. How else will you travel back two thousand years to the cross where Jesus' crucifixion took place? Faith is not blind nor is it foolishness as the world would have you believe. It is based upon truth and the Scriptures. Faith has the ability to transport you back two thousand years to his blood. Even the believers who accomplish very little for the kingdom of God are far wiser than the wisest of the world who insist on perishing. The psalmist writes: "Only fools say in their hearts, 'There is no God'" (Psalm 14:1). Do you count yourself a fool? Then, bow your knee before the Son of God, and acknowledge that he is God. And, if he is God, then it is your responsibility, privilege, and honor to seek after him. To seek after Jesus is to actively worship God. And, once you have found him, it is only the beginning. So faith plays an important role. In fact, "it is impossible to please God without faith" (Hebrews 11:6).

Every person who believes in Jesus has been given "the right to become children of God" (John 1:12). They have died to this world, and they have been translated into his kingdom. They are learning to travel a narrow road that leads to eternal life. It is so sad that so few ever find this road. Blessed are the ones who find it and then, with great determination, insist on traveling onward. For them, each day has become a daily adventure.

Jesus is the salvation of God. He is truth. There are no other pathways to God. Do not be deceived. God's reality is the only reality with a firm grip on eternity. Remember, the road to God is narrow. Always look up! He will return as he said he would. Jesus will burst forth from the clouds "with great power and glory" (Mark 13:26).

> "But cowards who turn away from me, and unbelievers, and the corrupt, and murderers, and the immoral, and those who practice witchcraft, and idol worshipers [worshippers], and all liars—their doom is in the lake that

I Am the Salvation of God

burns with fire and sulfur. This is the second death. (Revelation 21:8)

Jesus said: "I am the way, the truth, and the life. No one can come to the Father except through me" (John 14:6). Trust in Jesus. Dare to see the world and yourself through his eyes, and then you will understand. Come and know God's unfailing love. There is no deception within God's offer of love. Come find the freedom that has eluded the world for hundreds of years. Dare to stand in his love. Come!

Many would-be saviors have come and gone over the centuries, and the world is marked by their passage. Just look around at the many different religions we have today. They all claim to know how to reach God or how to attain the status of God. That was not Jesus. Jesus was completely different. He did not claim that he knew how to reach God or that he knew how to reach some spiritual state of complete fulfillment. No. That was not Jesus. Jesus claimed to be the "way," to be the "truth," and to be the "life." Jesus unquestionably declared himself to be God (McDowell, 1999, p. 150).

Jesus descended into our world, and through him we can ascend into his world. Is he your way? Is he your truth? Is he your life? These are all short questions, but they will have an eternal impact. Each of you must determine how you will respond to God's eternal provision. I hope you choose wisely. Remember the words, the deeds, and the death of Jesus Christ; they are all recorded in the one book from antiquity with the greatest amount of historical documentations. This was not done by accident. You may trust the Word of God, and you should trust in the work of the Son of God.

Bibliography

Alcorn, R. (2004). *Heaven*. Sandy, OR: Eternal Perspective Ministries/Tyndale House Publishers, Inc.

Bruce, F.F. (1983). *The Gospel of John: Introduction, Exposition, and Notes*. Grand Rapids, MI: Pickering & Inglis Ltd.

Chan, F. (2009). *Forgotten God: Reversing Our Tragic Neglect of the Holy Spirit*. Colorado Springs, CO: David Cook and D.C. Jacobson & Associates LLC.

Craig, W. L. (2008). *Reasonable Faith: Christian Truth and Apologetics*. Third Edition. Wheaton, IL: Crossway.

DeStefano, A. (2020). *Hell: A Guide*. Nashville, TN: Nelson Books.

Frazee, R. (2015). *Believe*. Grand Rapids, MI: Zondervan.

Ham, K. (2013). *Six Days: The Age of the Earth and the Decline of the Church*. Green Forest, AR: Master Books.

Jeffress, R. (2017). *A Place Called Heaven: 10 Surprising Truths about Your Eternal Home*. Grand Rapids, MI: Baker Books.

Jeremiah, D. (2016). *Is This the End? Signs of God's Providence in a Disturbing New World*. Nashville, TN: W Publishing Group.

Lewis, C. S. (1973). *The Great Divorce*. New York, NY: HarperCollins Publishers.

McDowell, J. (1999). *The New Evidence That Demands a Verdict.* Nashville, TN: Thomas Nelson, Inc., Publishers.

McGrath, A. E. (2011). *The Christian Theology Reader.* West Sussex, United Kingdom: Wiley-Blackwell Publishing.

Morris, L. (1971). *The Gospel According to John: The New International Commentary on the New Testament.* Grand Rapids, MI: WM. B. Eerdmans Publishing Co.

Pink, A. W. (2006). *The Attributes of God.* Grand Rapids, MI: Baker Books.

Sloyan, G. (1988). *John: Interpretation—A Bible Commentary for Teaching and Preaching.* Atlanta, GA: John Knox Press.

Tasker, R. V. G. (1960). *John: Tyndale—New Testament Commentaries.* Grand Rapids, MI: WM. B. Eerdmans Publishing Co.

Wiese, B. (2017). *23 Minutes in Hell: One Man's Story about What He Saw, Heard, and Felt in That Place of Torment.* Lake Mary, FL: Charisma House.

About the Author

STEPHEN BARBER HAS SERVED as a co-pastor, assistant pastor, and small group pastor. With a master's degree in Biblical Studies, he has racked up hundreds of hours studying the Bible. Stephen has never hesitated to examine controversial topics or issues that appeared to threaten the legitimacy of the Bible. Through these explorations, he gained an invaluable respect for the wisdom contained within God's Word.

Stephen has a sincere desire to provide people with the opportunity to make an informed decision about their eternal destiny. No one should step into eternity without knowing where that first step will lead them.

www.ingramcontent.com/pod-product-compliance
Lightning Source LLC
Chambersburg PA
CBHW061431040426
42450CB00007B/998